peace.
100 verses
for your
daily journey.

Freeman-Smith, a division of Worthy Media, Inc.
134 Franklin Road, Suite 200, Brentwood, Tennessee 37027

The quoted ideas expressed in this book (but not Scripture verses) are not, in all cases, exact quotations, as some have been edited for clarity and brevity. In all cases, the author has attempted to maintain the speaker's original intent. In some cases, quoted material for this book was obtained from secondary sources, primarily print media. While every effort was made to ensure the accuracy of these sources, the accuracy cannot be guaranteed. For additions, deletions, corrections, or clarifications in future editions of this text, please write Freeman-Smith.

Scripture quotations are taken from:

The Holy Bible, King James Version (KJV)

The Holy Bible, New International Version (NIV) Copyright © 1973, 1978, 1984, by International Bible Society. Used by permission of Zondervan Publishing House. All rights reserved.

The Holy Bible, New King James Version (NKJV) Copyright © 1982 by Thomas Nelson, Inc. Used by permission.

Holy Bible, New Living Translation, (NLT) copyright © 1996. Used by permission of Tyndale House Publishers, Inc., Wheaton, Illinois 60189. All rights reserved.

The Message (MSG)- This edition issued by contractual arrangement with NavPress, a division of The Navigators, U.S.A. Originally published by NavPress in English as THE MESSAGE: The Bible in Contemporary Language copyright 2002-2003 by Eugene Peterson. All rights reserved.

New Century Version®. (NCV) Copyright © 1987, 1988, 1991 by Word Publishing, a division of Thomas Nelson, Inc. All rights reserved. Used by permission.

The New American Standard Bible®, (NASB) Copyright © 1960, 1962, 1963, 1968, 1971, 1972, 1973, 1975, 1977, 1995 by The Lockman Foundation. Used by permission.

The Holman Christian Standard Bible™ (HCSB) Copyright © 1999, 2000, 2001 by Holman Bible Publishers. Used by permission.

Cover Design by Kim Russell / Wahoo Designs
Page Layout by Bart Dawson

ISBN 978-1-60587-352-7

Printed in the United States of America

peace.
100 verses
for your
daily journey.

Introduction

There are some Bible verses that are so important, so crucial to the Christian faith, that every believer should consider them carefully and review them often. This text examines 100 of the most familiar verses from God's Holy Word. These verses, which you've probably heard many times before, are short enough and memorable enough to provide courage for your daily journey. So do yourself and your loved ones a favor: study each verse and do your best to place it permanently in your mind and in your heart. When you do, you'll discover that having God's Word in your heart is even better than having a Bible on your bookshelf.

And the peace of God, which surpasses every thought, will guard your hearts and your minds in Christ Jesus. Finally brothers, whatever is true, whatever is honorable, whatever is just, whatever is pure, whatever is lovely, whatever is commendable—if there is any moral excellence and if there is any praise—dwell on these things.

Philippians 4:7-8 HCSB

Genuine Peace

Sometimes, peace can be a scarce commodity in a demanding, 21st-century world. How, then, can we find the peace that we so desperately desire? By turning our days and our lives over to God.

The Scottish preacher George McDonald observed, "It has been well said that no man ever sank under the burden of the day. It is when tomorrow's burden is added to the burden of today that the weight is more than a man can bear. Never load yourselves so, my friends. If you find yourselves so loaded, at least remember this: it is your own doing, not God's. He begs you to leave the future to Him."

May we give our lives, our hopes, our prayers, and our futures to the Father, and, by doing so, accept His will and His peace.

More Great Ideas About Peace

God has promised us abundance, peace, and eternal life. These treasures are ours for the asking; all we must do is claim them. One of the great mysteries of life is why on earth do so many of us wait so very long to claim them?

Marie T. Freeman

That peace, which has been described and which believers enjoy, is a participation of the peace which their glorious Lord and Master himself enjoys.

Jonathan Edwards

God's peace is like a river, not a pond. In other words, a sense of health and well-being, both of which are expressions of the Hebrew *shalom,* can permeate our homes even when we're in white-water rapids.

Beth Moore

When you and I are related to Jesus Christ, our strength and wisdom and peace and joy and love and hope may run out, but His life rushes in to keep us filled to the brim. We are showered with blessings, not because of anything we have or have not done, but simply because of Him.

Anne Graham Lotz

More from God's Word

If possible, on your part, live at peace with everyone.

Romans 12:18 HCSB

Abundant peace belongs to those who love Your instruction; nothing makes them stumble.

Psalm 119:165 HCSB

Blessed are the peacemakers, for they shall be called sons of God.

Matthew 5:9 NKJV

And suddenly there was with the angel a multitude of the heavenly host praising God and saying: "Glory to God in the highest, and on earth peace, goodwill toward men!"

Luke 2:13-14 NKJV

So then, we must pursue what promotes peace and what builds up one another.

Romans 14:19 HCSB

For God so loved the world, that he gave his only begotten Son, that whosoever believeth in him should not perish, but have everlasting life.

John 3:16 KJV

The Gift of Eternal Life

L et's review John 3:16, a verse that you've undoubtedly known since childhood. After all, this verse is, quite possibly, the most widely recognized sentence in the entire Bible. But even if you memorized this verse many years ago, you still need to make sure it's a verse that you can recite by heart now.

John 3:16 makes this promise: If you believe in Jesus, you will live forever with Him in heaven. It's an amazing promise, and it's the cornerstone of the Christian faith.

Eternal life is not an event that begins when you die. Eternal life begins when you invite Jesus into your heart right here on earth. So it's important to remember that God's plans for you are not limited to the ups and downs of everyday life. If you've allowed Jesus to reign over your heart, you've already begun your eternal journey.

As mere mortals, our vision for the future, like our lives here on earth, is limited. God's vision is not burdened by such limitations: His plans extend throughout all eternity.

Let us praise the Creator for His priceless gift, and let us share the Good News with all who cross our paths. We return our Father's love by accepting His grace and by sharing His message and His love. When we do, we are blessed here on earth and throughout all eternity.

More Great Ideas About Eternal Life

Like a shadow declining swiftly...away...like the dew of the morning gone with the heat of the day; like the wind in the treetops, like a wave of the sea, so are our lives on earth when seen in light of eternity.

Ruth Bell Graham

God's salvation comes as gift; it is eternal, and it is a continuum, meaning it starts when I receive the gift in faith and is never-ending.

Franklin Graham

All that is not eternal is eternally out of date.

C. S. Lewis

Let us see the victorious Jesus, the conqueror of the tomb, the one who defied death. And let us be reminded that we, too, will be granted the same victory.

Max Lucado

More from God's Word

And this is the testimony: God has given us eternal life, and this life is in His Son. The one who has the Son has life. The one who doesn't have the Son of God does not have life.

1 John 5:11-12 HCSB

And this is the will of Him who sent Me, that everyone who sees the Son and believes in Him may have everlasting life; and I will raise him up at the last day.

John 6:40 NKJV

Pursue righteousness, godliness, faith, love, endurance, and gentleness. Fight the good fight for the faith; take hold of eternal life, to which you were called and have made a good confession before many witnesses.

1 Timothy 6:11-12 HCSB

Jesus said to her, "I am the resurrection and the life. The one who believes in Me, even if he dies, will live. Everyone who lives and believes in Me will never die—ever. Do you believe this?"

John 11:25-26 HCSB

In a little while the world will see Me no longer, but you will see Me. Because I live, you will live too.

John 14:19 HCSB

The Lord is my shepherd; I shall not want. He makes me to lie down in green pastures; He leads me beside the still waters. He restores my soul.

Psalm 23:1-3 NKJV

God's Protection

David, the author of the 23rd Psalm, realized that God was his shield, his protector, and his salvation. And if we're wise, we realize it, too. After all, God has promised to protect us, and He intends to keep His promise.

In a world filled with dangers and temptations, God is the ultimate armor. In a world filled with misleading messages, God's Word is the ultimate truth. In a world filled with more frustrations than we can count, God's Son offers the ultimate peace.

Will you accept God's peace and wear God's armor against the dangers of our world? Hopefully so—because when you do, you can live courageously, knowing that you possess the supreme protection: God's unfailing love for you.

The world offers no safety nets, but God does. He sent His only begotten Son to offer you the priceless gift of eternal life. And now you are challenged to return

God's love by obeying His commandments and honoring His Son.

Sometimes, in the crush of everyday life, God may seem far away, but He is not. God is everywhere you have ever been and everywhere you will ever go. He is with you night and day; He knows your thoughts and your prayers. And, when you earnestly seek His protection, you will find it because He is here—always—waiting patiently for you to reach out to Him. And the next move, of course, is yours.

More Great Ideas About God's Protection

We sometimes fear to bring our troubles to God because we think they must seem small to Him. But, if they are large enough to vex and endanger our welfare, they are large enough to touch His heart of love.

R. A. Torrey

God does not promise to keep us out of the storms and floods, but He does promise to sustain us in the storm, and then bring us out in due time for His glory when the storm has done its work.

Warren Wiersbe

More from God's Word

I know whom I have believed and am persuaded that He is able to guard what has been entrusted to me until that day.

2 Timothy 1:12 HCSB

For the LORD your God has arrived to live among you. He is a mighty savior. He will rejoice over you with great gladness. With his love, he will calm all your fears. He will exult over you by singing a happy song.

Zephaniah 3:17 HCSB

In all your ways acknowledge Him, and He shall direct your paths.

Proverbs 3:6 NKJV

Don't worry about your life, what you will eat or what you will drink; or about your body, what you will wear. Isn't life more than food and the body more than clothing?

Matthew 6:25 HCSB

Don't worry about anything, but in everything, through prayer and petition with thanksgiving, let your requests be made known to God.

Philippians 4:6 HCSB

And now abide faith, hope, love, these three; but the greatest of these is love.

1 Corinthians 13:13 NKJV

The Greatest of These Is Love

The familiar words of 1st Corinthians 13 remind us of the importance of love. Faith is important, of course. So, too, is hope. But love is more important still.

Christ showed His love for us on the cross, and, as Christians, we are called upon to return Christ's love by sharing it. We are commanded (not advised, not encouraged…commanded!) to love one another just as Christ loved us (John 13:34). That's a tall order, but as Christians, we are obligated to follow it.

Sometimes love is easy (puppies and sleeping children come to mind) and sometimes love is hard (fallible human beings come to mind). But God's Word is clear: We are to love our all our friends and neighbors, not just the lovable ones. So today, take time to spread Christ's message by word and by example. And the greatest of these is, of course, example.

More Great Ideas About Love

Live your lives in love, the same sort of love which Christ gives us, and which He perfectly expressed when He gave Himself as a sacrifice to God.

Corrie ten Boom

Suppose that I understand the Bible. And, suppose that I am the greatest preacher who ever lived! The Apostle Paul wrote that unless I have love, "I am nothing."

Billy Graham

Carve your name on hearts, not on marble.

C. H. Spurgeon

How do you spell love? When you reach the point where the happiness, security, and development of another person is as much of a driving force to you as your own happiness, security, and development, then you have a mature love. True love is spelled G-I-V-E. It is not based on what you can get, but rooted in what you can give to the other person.

Josh McDowell

He who is filled with love is filled with God Himself.

St. Augustine

More from God's Word

Beloved, if God so loved us, we also ought to love one another.

1 John 4:11 NASB

The one who loves his brother remains in the light, and there is no cause for stumbling in him.

1 John 2:10 HCSB

Now these three remain: faith, hope, and love. But the greatest of these is love.

1 Corinthians 13:13 HCSB

No one has ever seen God. If we love one another, God remains in us and His love is perfected in us.

1 John 4:12 HCSB

And we have this command from Him: the one who loves God must also love his brother.

1 John 4:21 HCSB

I am come that they might have life, and that they might have it more abundantly.

John 10:10 KJV

Accepting God's Abundance

The 10th chapter of John tells us that Christ came to earth so that our lives might be filled with abundance. But what, exactly, did Jesus mean when He promised "life…more abundantly"? Was He referring to material possessions or financial wealth? Hardly. Jesus offers a different kind of abundance: a spiritual richness that extends beyond the temporal boundaries of this world.

Is material abundance part of God's plan for our lives? Perhaps. But in every circumstance of life, during times of wealth or times of want, God will provide us what we need if we trust Him (Matthew 6). May we, as believers, claim the riches of Christ Jesus every day that we live, and may we share His blessings with all who cross our path.

More Great Ideas About Abundance

Jesus intended for us to be overwhelmed by the blessings of regular days. He said it was the reason he had come: "I am come that they might have life, and that they might have it more abundantly."

Gloria Gaither

Jesus wants Life for us, Life with a capital L.

John Eldredge

The Bible says that being a Christian is not only a great way to die, but it's also the best way to live.

Bill Hybels

People, places, and things were never meant to give us life. God alone is the author of a fulfilling life.

Gary Smalley & John Trent

God loves you and wants you to experience peace and life—abundant and eternal.

Billy Graham

More from God's Word

Until now you have asked for nothing in My name. Ask and you will receive, that your joy may be complete.

John 16:24 HCSB

And God is able to make every grace overflow to you, so that in every way, always having everything you need, you may excel in every good work.

2 Corinthians 9:8 HCSB

Come to terms with God and be at peace; in this way good will come to you.

Job 22:21 HCSB

My cup runs over. Surely goodness and mercy shall follow me all the days of my life; and I will dwell in the house of the Lord forever.

Psalm 23:5-6 NKJV

And He said to them, "Take heed and beware of covetousness, for one's life does not consist in the abundance of the things he possesses."

Luke 12:15 NKJV

21

I am the vine, you are the branches. He who abides in Me, and I in him, bears much fruit; for without Me you can do nothing.

John 15:5 NKJV

He Is the Vine

He was the Son of God, but He wore a crown of thorns. He was the Savior of mankind, yet He was put to death on a roughhewn wooden cross. He offered His healing touch to an unsaved world, and yet the same hands that had healed the sick and raised the dead were pierced with nails.

Jesus Christ, the Son of God, was born into humble circumstances. He walked this earth, not as a ruler of men, but as the Savior of mankind. His crucifixion, a torturous punishment that was intended to end His life and His reign, instead became the pivotal event in the history of all humanity. Christ sacrificed His life on the cross so that we might have eternal life. This gift, freely given by God's only begotten Son, is the priceless possession of everyone who accepts Him as Lord and Savior.

Why did Christ endure the humiliation and torture of the cross? He did it for you. His love is as near as your next breath, as personal as your next thought, more essential than your next heartbeat. And what must you do in response to the Savior's gifts? You must accept His love, praise His name, and share His message of salvation. And, you must conduct yourself in a manner that demonstrates to all the world that your acquaintance with the Master is not a passing fancy but that it is, instead, the cornerstone and the touchstone of your life.

More Great Ideas About Jesus

In your greatest weakness, turn to your greatest strength, Jesus, and hear Him say, "My grace is sufficient for you, for My strength is made perfect in weakness" (2 Corinthians 12:9 NKJV).

Lisa Whelchel

There is not a single thing that Jesus cannot change, control, and conquer because He is the living Lord.

Franklin Graham

When you can't see him, trust him. Jesus is closer than you ever dreamed.

Max Lucado

Sold for thirty pieces of silver, he redeemed the world.

R. G. Lee

More from God's Word

I am the door. If anyone enters by Me, he will be saved.

John 10:9 NKJV

I have come as a light into the world, so that everyone who believes in Me would not remain in darkness.

John 12:46 HCSB

We have seen it and we testify and declare to you the eternal life that was with the Father and was revealed to us—what we have seen and heard we also declare to you, so that you may have fellowship along with us; and indeed our fellowship is with the Father and with His Son Jesus Christ.

1 John 1:2-4 HCSB

Jesus Christ is the same yesterday, today, and forever.

Hebrews 13:8 HCSB

But we do see Jesus—made lower than the angels for a short time so that by God's grace He might taste death for everyone—crowned with glory and honor because of the suffering of death.

Hebrews 2:9 HCSB

Ask, and it will be given to you; seek, and you will find; knock, and it will be opened to you. For everyone who asks receives, and he who seeks finds, and to him who knocks it will be opened.

Matthew 7:7-8 NKJV

Ask Him for the Things You Need

How often do you ask God for His help and His wisdom? Occasionally? Intermittently? Whenever you experience a crisis? Hopefully not. Hopefully, you've acquired the habit of asking for God's assistance early and often. And hopefully, you have learned to seek His guidance in every aspect of your life.

In Matthew 7, God promises that He will guide you if you let Him. Your job is to let Him. But sometimes, you will be tempted to do otherwise. Sometimes, you'll be tempted to go along with the crowd; other times, you'll be tempted to do things your way, not God's way. When you feel those temptations, resist them.

God has promised that when you ask for His help, He will not withhold it. So ask. Ask Him to meet the needs of your day. Ask Him to lead you, to protect you, and to correct you. And trust the answers He gives.

God stands at the door and waits. When you knock, He opens. When you ask, He answers. Your task, of course, is to seek His guidance prayerfully, confidently, and often.

More Great Ideas About Asking God

God makes prayer as easy as possible for us. He's completely approachable and available, and He'll never mock or upbraid us for bringing our needs before Him.

Shirley Dobson

Don't be afraid to ask your heavenly Father for anything you need. Indeed, nothing is too small for God's attention or too great for his power.

Dennis Swanberg

Notice that we must ask. And we will sometimes struggle to hear and struggle with what we hear. But personally, it's worth it. I'm after the path of life—and he alone knows it.

John Eldredge

God's help is always available, but it is only given to those who seek it.

Max Lucado

More from God's Word

Don't worry about anything, but in everything, through prayer and petition with thanksgiving, let your requests be made known to God.

Philippians 4:6 HCSB

If you remain in Me and My words remain in you, ask whatever you want and it will be done for you.

John 15:7 HCSB

What father among you, if his son asks for a fish, will, instead of a fish, give him a snake? Or if he asks for an egg, will give him a scorpion? If you then, who are evil, know how to give good gifts to your children, how much more will the heavenly Father give the Holy Spirit to those who ask Him?

Luke 11:11-13 HCSB

So I say to you, keep asking, and it will be given to you. Keep searching, and you will find. Keep knocking, and the door will be opened to you.

Luke 11:9 HCSB

You do not have because you do not ask.

James 4:2 HCSB

*This is the day which the LORD hath made; we will rejoice
and be glad in it.*

Psalm 118:24 KJV

Celebrate the Gift of Life

Today is a non-renewable resource—once it's
gone, it's gone forever. Our responsibility, as
thoughtful believers, is to use this day in the
service of God's will and in the service of His people.
When we do so, we enrich our own lives and the lives of
those whom we love.

God has richly blessed us, and He wants you to rejoice in His gifts. That's why this day—and each day
that follows—should be a time of prayer and celebration
as we consider the Good News of God's free gift: salvation through Jesus Christ.

Oswald Chambers correctly observed, "Joy is the
great note all throughout the Bible." E. Stanley Jones
echoed that thought when he wrote, "Christ and joy go
together." But, even the most dedicated Christians can,
on occasion, forget to celebrate each day for what it is: a
priceless gift from God.

What do you expect from the day ahead? Are you
expecting God to do wonderful things, or are you living

beneath a cloud of apprehension and doubt? The familiar words of Psalm 118:24 remind us that every day is a cause for celebration. Our duty, as believers, is to rejoice in God's marvelous creation.

Today, celebrate the life that God has given you. Today, put a smile on your face, kind words on your lips, and a song in your heart. Be generous with your praise and free with your encouragement. And then, when you have celebrated life to the fullest, invite your friends to do likewise. After all, this is God's day, and He has given us clear instructions for its use. We are commanded to rejoice and be glad.

More Great Ideas About Joyful Living

Christ is the secret, the source, the substance, the center, and the circumference of all true and lasting gladness.

Mrs. Charles E. Cowman

Now is the only time worth having because, indeed, it is the only time we have.

C. H. Spurgeon

Yesterday is the tomb of time, and tomorrow is the womb of time. Only now is yours.

R. G. Lee

More from God's Word

I must work the works of Him who sent Me while it is day; the night is coming when no one can work.

John 9:4 NKJV

Working together with Him, we also appeal to you: "Don't receive God's grace in vain." For He says: In an acceptable time, I heard you, and in the day of salvation, I helped you. Look, now is the acceptable time; look, now is the day of salvation.

2 Corinthians 6:1-2 HCSB

Therefore, get your minds ready for action, being self-disciplined, and set your hope completely on the grace to be brought to you at the revelation of Jesus Christ.

1 Peter 1:13 HCSB

Rejoice in the Lord always. I will say it again: Rejoice!

Philippians 4:4 HCSB

So teach us to number our days, that we may gain a heart of wisdom.

Psalm 90:12 NKJV

After this manner therefore pray ye: Our Father which art in heaven, Hallowed be thy name. Thy kingdom come. Thy will be done in earth, as it is in heaven. Give us this day our daily bread. And forgive us our debts, as we forgive our debtors. And lead us not into temptation, but deliver us from evil: For thine is the kingdom, and the power, and the glory, for ever. Amen

Matthew 6:9-13 KJV

The Lord's Prayer

"Our Father which art in heaven, hallowed be thy name." These familiar words begin the Lord's Prayer, a prayer that you've heard on countless occasions. It's the prayer that Jesus taught His followers to pray, and it's a prayer that you probably know by heart.

You already know what the prayer says, but have you thought carefully, and in detail, about exactly what those words mean? Hopefully so. After all, this simple prayer was authored by Savior of mankind.

Today, take the time to carefully consider each word in this beautiful passage. When you weave thes Lord's Prayer into the fabric of your life, you'll soon discover that God's Word and God's Son have the power to change everything, including you.

More Great Ideas About God

When all else is gone, God is left, and nothing changes Him.

Hannah Whitall Smith

God is an infinite circle whose center is everywhere and whose circumference is nowhere.

St. Augustine

The God who dwells in heaven is willing to dwell also in the heart of the humble believer.

Warren Wiersbe

A sense of deity is inscribed on every heart.

John Calvin

God's actual divine essence and His will are absolutely beyond all human thought, human understanding or wisdom; in short, they are and ever will be incomprehensible, inscrutable, and altogether hidden to human reason.

Martin Luther

More from God's Word

Help me, Lord my God; save me according to Your faithful love.

Psalm 109:26 HCSB

The LORD is my strength and song, and He has become my salvation; He is my God, and I will praise Him…

Exodus 15:2 NKJV

Peace, peace to you, and peace to your helpers! For your God helps you.

1 Chronicles 12:18 NKJV

He gives power to the weak, and to those who have no might He increases strength.

Isaiah 40:29 NKJV

Therefore whoever hears these sayings of Mine, and does them, I will liken him to a wise man who built his house on the rock: and the rain descended, the floods came, and the winds blew and beat on that house; and it did not fall, for it was founded on the rock.

Matthew 7:24-25 NKJV

Therefore, whatever you want others to do for you, do also the same for them—this is the Law and the Prophets.

Matthew 7:12 HCSB

The Golden Rule

The words of Matthew 7:12 remind us that, as believers in Christ, we are commanded to treat others as we wish to be treated. This commandment is, indeed, the Golden Rule for Christians of every generation. When we weave the thread of kindness into the very fabric of our lives, we give glory to the One who gave His life for ours.

Because we are imperfect human beings, we are, on occasion, selfish, thoughtless, or cruel. But God commands us to behave otherwise. He teaches us to rise above our own imperfections and to treat others with unselfishness and love. When we observe God's Golden Rule, we help build His kingdom here on earth. And, when we share the love of Christ, we share a priceless gift; may we share it today and every day that we live.

More Great Ideas About the Golden Rule

In your desire to share the gospel, you may be the only Jesus someone else will ever meet. Be real and be involved with people.

Barbara Johnson

Love is not grabbing, or self-centered, or selfish. Real love is being able to contribute to the happiness of another person without expecting to get anything in return.

James Dobson

When you extend hospitality to others, you're not trying to impress people, you're trying to reflect God to them.

Max Lucado

Be so preoccupied with good will that you haven't room for ill will.

E. Stanley Jones

The golden rule to follow to obtain spiritual understanding is not one of intellectual pursuit, but one of obedience.

Oswald Chambers

More from God's Word

So we must not get tired of doing good, for we will reap at the proper time if we don't give up.

Galatians 6:9 HCSB

See that no one renders evil for evil to anyone, but always pursue what is good both for yourselves and for all.

1 Thessalonians 5:15 NKJV

If you really carry out the royal law prescribed in Scripture, You shall love your neighbor as yourself, you are doing well.

James 2:8 HCSB

Finally, all of you be of one mind, having compassion for one another; love as brothers, be tenderhearted, be courteous.

1 Peter 3:8 NKJV

And be kind and compassionate to one another, forgiving one another, just as God also forgave you in Christ.

Ephesians 4:32 HCSB

Cast thy burden upon the LORD, and he shall sustain thee: he shall never suffer the righteous to be moved.

Psalm 55:22 KJV

Where to Place Your Burdens

God's Word contains promises upon which we, as Christians, can and must depend. The Bible is a priceless gift, a tool that God intends for us to use in every aspect of our lives. Too many Christians, however, keep their spiritual tool kits tightly closed and out of sight.

Psalm 55:22 instructs us to cast our burdens upon the Lord. And that's perfect advice for men, women, and children alike.

Are you tired? Discouraged? Fearful? Be comforted and trust the promises that God has made to you. Are you worried or anxious? Be confident in God's power. He will never desert you. Do you see a difficult future ahead? Be courageous and call upon God. He will protect you and then use you according to His purposes. Are you confused? Listen to the quiet voice of your Heavenly Father. He is not a God of confusion. Talk with Him; listen to Him; trust Him, and trust His promises.

More Great Ideas About God's Support

Once we recognize our need for Jesus, then the building of our faith begins. It is a daily, moment-by-moment life of absolute dependence upon Him for everything.

Catherine Marshall

When you have no helpers, see all your helpers in God. When you have many helpers, see God in all your helpers. When you have nothing but God, see all in God; when you have everything, see God in everything. Under all conditions, stay thy heart only on the Lord.

C. H. Spurgeon

We have ample evidence that the Lord is able to guide. The promises cover every imaginable situation. All we need to do is to take the hand he stretches out.

Elisabeth Elliot

Measure the size of the obstacles against the size of God.

Beth Moore

Faith is not merely you holding on to God—it is God holding on to you.

E. Stanley Jones

More from God's Word

Now the God of all grace, who called you to His eternal glory in Christ Jesus, will personally restore, establish, strengthen, and support you.

1 Peter 5:10 HCSB

Peace, peace to you, and peace to your helpers! For your God helps you.

1 Chronicles 12:18 NKJV

He gives power to the weak, and to those who have no might He increases strength.

Isaiah 40:29 NKJV

Therefore whoever hears these sayings of Mine, and does them, I will liken him to a wise man who built his house on the rock: and the rain descended, the floods came, and the winds blew and beat on that house; and it did not fall, for it was founded on the rock.

Matthew 7:24-25 NKJV

I am able to do all things through Him who strengthens me.

Philippians 4:13 HCSB

But grow in the grace and knowledge of our Lord and Savior Jesus Christ. To Him be the glory both now and forever.

2 Peter 3:18 NKJV

Spiritual Growth

The words of 2 Peter 3:18 make it clear: spiritual growth is a journey, not a destination. When it comes to your faith, God doesn't intend for you to stand still; He wants you to keep moving and growing. In fact, God's plan for you includes a lifetime of prayer, praise, and spiritual growth.

Many of life's most important lessons are painful to learn. During times of heartbreak and hardship, we must be courageous and we must be patient, knowing that in His own time, God will heal us if we invite Him into our hearts.

Spiritual growth need not take place only in times of adversity. We must seek to grow in our knowledge and love of the Lord every day that we live. In those quiet moments when we open our hearts to God, the One who made us keeps remaking us. He gives us direction, perspective, wisdom, and courage. The appropriate moment to accept those spiritual gifts is the present one.

Are you as mature as you're ever going to be? Hopefully not! When it comes to your faith, God doesn't intend for you to become "fully grown," at least not in this lifetime. In fact, God still has important lessons that He intends to teach you. So ask yourself this: what lesson is God trying to teach me today? And then go about the business of learning it.

More Great Ideas About Spiritual Growth

You are either becoming more like Christ every day or you're becoming less like Him. There is no neutral position in the Lord.

Stormie Omartian

God's plan for our guidance is for us to grow gradually in wisdom before we get to the crossroads.

Bill Hybels

A person who gazes and keeps on gazing at Jesus becomes like him in appearance.

E. Stanley Jones

We often become mentally and spiritually barren because we're so busy.

Franklin Graham

More from God's Word

For this reason also, since the day we heard this, we haven't stopped praying for you. We are asking that you may be filled with the knowledge of His will in all wisdom and spiritual understanding.

Colossians 1:9 HCSB

I want their hearts to be encouraged and joined together in love, so that they may have all the riches of assured understanding, and have the knowledge of God's mystery— Christ.

Colossians 2:2 HCSB

Therefore, leaving the elementary message about the Messiah, let us go on to maturity.

Hebrews 6:1 HCSB

For You, O God, have tested us; You have refined us as silver is refined. You brought us into the net; You laid affliction on our backs. You have caused men to ride over our heads; we went through fire and through water; but You brought us out to rich fulfillment.

Psalm 66:10–12 NKJV

*But those who wait on the Lord shall renew their strength;
they shall mount up with wings like eagles, they shall run and
not be weary, they shall walk and not faint.*

Isaiah 40:31 NKJV

Strength from God

E ven the most inspired Christians can, from time
to time, find themselves running on empty. The
demands of daily life can drain us of our strength
and rob us of the joy that is rightfully ours in Christ.
When we find ourselves tired, discouraged, or worse,
there is a source from which we can draw the power
needed to recharge our spiritual batteries. That source
is God.

God intends that His children lead joyous lives
filled with abundance and peace. But sometimes, abundance and peace seem very far away. It is then that we
must turn to God for renewal, and when we do, He will
restore us if we allow Him to do so.

Today, like every other day, is literally brimming
with possibilities. Whether we realize it or not, God is
always working in us and through us; our job is to let
Him do His work without undue interference. Yet we
are imperfect beings who, because of our limited vision,
often resist God's will. And oftentimes, because of our

stubborn insistence on squeezing too many activities into a 24-hour day, we allow ourselves to become exhausted, or frustrated, or both.

Are you tired or troubled? Turn your heart toward God in prayer. Are you weak or worried? Take the time—or, more accurately, make the time—to delve deeply into God's Holy Word. Are you spiritually depleted? Call upon fellow believers to support you, and call upon Christ to renew your spirit and your life. Are you simply overwhelmed by the demands of the day? Pray for the wisdom to simplify your life. Are you exhausted? Pray for the wisdom to rest a little more and worry a little less.

When you do these things, you'll discover that the Creator of the universe stands always ready and always able to create a new sense of wonderment and joy in you.

The Lord is my strength and my song; He has become my salvation.

—

Exodus 15:2 HCSB

More Great Ideas About Strength

Worry does not empty tomorrow of its sorrow; it empties today of its strength.

Corrie ten Boom

If we take God's program, we can have God's power—not otherwise.

E. Stanley Jones

One reason so much American Christianity is a mile wide and an inch deep is that Christians are simply tired. Sometimes you need to kick back and rest for Jesus' sake.

Dennis Swanberg

We have a God who delights in impossibilities.

Andrew Murray

The same God who empowered Samson, Gideon, and Paul seeks to empower my life and your life, because God hasn't changed.

Bill Hybels

Be still, and know that I am God....

Psalm 46:10 KJV

Be Still

We live in a noisy world, a world filled with distractions, frustrations, obligations, and complications. But we must not allow our clamorous world to separate us from God's peace. Instead, we must "be still" so that we might sense the presence of God.

If we are to maintain righteous minds and compassionate hearts, we must take time each day for prayer and for meditation. We must make ourselves still in the presence of our Creator. We must quiet our minds and our hearts so that we might sense God's love, God's will, and God's Son.

Has the busy pace of life robbed you of the peace that might otherwise be yours through Jesus Christ? If so, it's time to reorder your priorities. Nothing is more important than the time you spend with your Savior. So be still and claim the inner peace that is your spiritual birthright: the peace of Jesus Christ. It is offered freely; it has been paid for in full; it is yours for the asking. So ask. And then share.

More Great Ideas About Quiet Time

When frustrations develop into problems that stress you out, the best way to cope is to stop, catch your breath, and do something for yourself, not out of selfishness, but out of wisdom.

Barbara Johnson

That is the source of Jeremiah's living persistence, his creative constancy. He was up before the sun, listening to God's word. Rising early, he was quiet and attentive before his Lord. Long before the yelling started, the mocking, the complaining, there was this centering, discovering, exploring time with God.

Eugene Peterson

Quiet time is giving God your undivided attention for a predetermined amount of time for the purpose of talking to and hearing from Him.

Charles Stanley

Let this be your chief object in prayer, to realize the presence of your heavenly Father. Let your watchword be: Alone with God.

Andrew Murray

But seek first the kingdom of God and His righteousness, and all these things shall be added to you. Therefore do not worry about tomorrow, for tomorrow will worry about its own things. Sufficient for the day is its own trouble.

Matthew 6:33-34 NKJV

Beyond Worry

B ecause we are imperfect human beings struggling with imperfect circumstances, we worry. Even though we, as Christians, have the assurance of salvation—even though we, as Christians, have the promise of God's love and protection—we find ourselves fretting over the inevitable frustrations of everyday life. Jesus understood our concerns when He spoke the reassuring words found in the 6th chapter of Matthew.

Where is the best place to take your worries? Take them to God. Take your troubles to Him; take your fears to Him; take your doubts to Him; take your weaknesses to Him; take your sorrows to Him . . . and leave them all there. Seek protection from the One who offers you eternal salvation; build your spiritual house upon the Rock that cannot be moved.

Perhaps you are concerned about your future, your health, or your finances. Or perhaps you are simply a "worrier" by nature. If so, make Matthew 6 a regular part of your daily Bible reading. This beautiful passage will remind you that God still sits in His heaven and you are His beloved child. Then, perhaps, you will worry a little less and trust God a little more, and that's as it should be because God is trustworthy . . . and you are protected.

More Great Ideas About Worry

Today is mine. Tomorrow is none of my business. If I peer anxiously into the fog of the future, I will strain my spiritual eyes so that I will not see clearly what is required of me now.

Elisabeth Elliott

Today is the tomorrow we worried about yesterday.

Dennis Swanberg

Worry and anxiety are sand in the machinery of life; faith is the oil.

E. Stanley Jones

Much that worries us beforehand can, quite unexpectedly, have a happy and simple solution. Worries just don't matter. Things really are in a better hand than ours.

Dietrich Bonhoeffer

More from God's Word

Those who trust in the Lord are like Mount Zion. It cannot be shaken; it remains forever.

Psalm 125:1 HCSB

Don't worry about anything, but in everything, through prayer and petition with thanksgiving, let your requests be made known to God.

Philippians 4:6 HCSB

Your heart must not be troubled. Believe in God; believe also in Me.

John 14:1 HCSB

Come to Me, all you who labor and are heavy laden, and I will give you rest. Take My yoke upon you and learn from Me, for I am gentle and lowly in heart, and you will find rest for your souls. For My yoke is easy and My burden is light.

Matthew 11:28-30 NKJV

I will be with you when you pass through the waters . . . when you walk through the fire . . . the flame will not burn you. For I the Lord your God, the Holy One of Israel, and your Savior.

Isaiah 43:2-3 HCSB

Trust in the Lord with all your heart, and lean not on your own understanding; in all your ways acknowledge Him, and He shall direct your paths.

Proverbs 3:5-6 NKJV

Trust Him

It's easy to talk about trusting God, but when it comes to actually trusting Him, that's considerably harder. Why? Because genuine trust in God requires more than words; it requires a willingness to follow God's lead and a willingness to obey His commandments. (These, by the way, are not easy things to do.)

Have you spent more time talking about Christ than walking in His footsteps? If so, God wants to have a little chat with you. And, if you're unwilling to talk to Him, He may take other actions in order to grab your attention.

Thankfully, whenever you're willing to talk with God, He's willing to listen. And, the instant that you decide to place Him squarely in the center of your life, He will respond to that decision with blessings that are too unexpected to predict and too numerous to count.

The next time you find your courage tested to the limit, lean upon God's promises. Trust His Son. Always remember that God is always near and that He is your protector and your deliverer. When you are worried, anxious, or afraid, call upon Him. God can handle your troubles infinitely better than you can, so turn them over to Him. Remember that God rules both mountain-tops and valleys—with limitless wisdom and love—now and forever.

The one who understands a matter finds success, and the one who trusts in the Lord will be happy.

—

Proverbs 16:20 HCSB

More Great Ideas About Trusting God

Are you serious about wanting God's guidance to become the person he wants you to be? The first step is to tell God that you know you can't manage your own life; that you need his help.

Catherine Marshall

Beware of trusting in yourself, and see that you trust in the Lord.

Oswald Chambers

The hope we have in Jesus is the anchor for the soul—something sure and steadfast, preventing drifting or giving way, lowered to the depth of God's love.

Franklin Graham

Trustfulness is based on confidence in God whose ways I do not understand.

Oswald Chambers

God is God. He knows what he is doing. When you can't trace his hand, trust his heart.

Max Lucado

For by grace you are saved through faith, and this is not from yourselves; it is God's gift—not from works, so that no one can boast.

Ephesians 2:8-9 HCSB

The Gift of Grace

In the second chapter of Ephesians, God promises that we will be saved by faith, not by works. It's no wonder, then, that someone once said that GRACE stands for God's Redemption At Christ's Expense. It's true—God sent His Son so that we might be redeemed from our sins. In doing so, our Heavenly Father demonstrated His infinite mercy and His infinite love. We have received countless gifts from God, but none can compare with the gift of salvation. God's grace is the ultimate gift, and we owe Him the ultimate in thanksgiving.

The gift of eternal life is the priceless possession of everyone who accepts God's Son as Lord and Savior. We return our Savior's love by welcoming Him into our hearts and sharing His message and His love. When we do so, we are blessed not today and forever.

More Great Ideas About Grace

How beautiful it is to learn that grace isn't fragile, and that in the family of God we can fail and not be a failure.

Gloria Gaither

Grace is but glory begun, and glory is but grace perfected.

Jonathan Edwards

Faith is a living, daring confidence in God's grace, so sure and certain that a man would stake his life on it a thousand times.

Martin Luther

The cross was heavy, the blood was real, and the price was extravagant. It would have bankrupted you or me, so he paid it for us. Call it simple. Call it a gift. But don't call it easy. Call it what it is. Call it grace.

Max Lucado

No one is beyond his grace. No situation, anywhere on earth, is too hard for God.

Jim Cymbala

More from God's Word

For the law was given through Moses; grace and truth came through Jesus Christ.

John 1:17 HCSB

Therefore let us approach the throne of grace with boldness, so that we may receive mercy and find grace to help us at the proper time.

Hebrews 4:16 HCSB

Therefore, since we are receiving a kingdom that cannot be shaken, let us hold on to grace. By it, we may serve God acceptably, with reverence and awe.

Hebrews 12:28 HCSB

You, therefore, my child, be strong in the grace that is in Christ Jesus.

2 Timothy 2:1 HCSB

For the grace of God has appeared, with salvation for all people, instructing us to deny godlessness and worldly lusts and to live in a sensible, righteous, and godly way in the present age.

Titus 2:11-12 HCSB

You will show me the path of life; in Your presence is fullness of joy; at Your right hand are pleasures forevermore.

Psalm 16:11 NKJV

He Will Show You the Path

Life is best lived on purpose. And purpose, like everything else in the universe, begins in the heart of God. Whether you realize it or not, God has a direction for your life, a divine calling, a path along which He intends to lead you. When you welcome God into your heart and establish a genuine relationship with Him, He will begin—and He will continue—to make His purposes known.

Each morning, as the sun rises in the east, you welcome a new day, one that is filled to the brim with opportunities, with possibilities, and with God. As you contemplate God's blessings in your own life, you should prayerfully seek His guidance for the day ahead.

Discovering God's unfolding purpose for your life is a daily journey, a journey guided by the teachings of God's Holy Word. As you reflect upon God's promises and upon the meaning that those promises hold for you, ask God to lead you throughout the coming day. Let your Heavenly Father direct your steps; concentrate on what God wants you to do now, and leave the distant future in hands that are far more capable than your own: His hands.

Sometimes, God's intentions will be clear to you; other times, God's plan will seem uncertain at best. But even on those difficult days when you are unsure which way to turn, you must never lose sight of these overriding facts: God created you for a reason; He has important work for you to do; and He's waiting patiently for you to do it. So why not begin today?

*I will instruct you and show you
the way to go; with My eye on you,
I will give counsel.*

—

Psalm 32:8 HCSB

More Great Ideas About Living on Purpose

How much of our lives are, well, so daily. How often our hours are filled with the mundane, seemingly unimportant things that have to be done, whether at home or work. These very "daily" tasks could become a celebration of praise. "It is through consecration," someone has said, "that drudgery is made divine."

Gigi Graham Tchividjian

Without God, life has no purpose, and without purpose, life has no meaning.

Rick Warren

Whatever purpose motivates your life, it must be something big enough and grand enough to make the investment worthwhile.

Warren Wiersbe

The worst thing that laziness does is rob a man of spiritual purpose.

Billy Graham

Continually restate to yourself what the purpose of your life is.

Oswald Chambers

Now by this we know that we know Him, if we keep His commandments.

1 John 2:3 NKJV

Obedience Now

Obedience to God is determined, not by words, but by deeds. Talking about righteousness is easy; living righteously is far more difficult, especially in today's temptation-filled world.

Since God created Adam and Eve, we human beings have been rebelling against our Creator. Why? Because we are unwilling to trust God's Word, and we are unwilling to follow His commandments. God has given us a guidebook for righteous living called the Holy Bible. It contains thorough instructions which, if followed, lead to fulfillment, abundance, and salvation. But, if we choose to ignore God's commandments, the results are as predictable as they are tragic.

When we seek righteousness in our own lives—and when we seek the companionship of those who do likewise—we reap the spiritual rewards that God intends for our lives. When we behave ourselves as godly men and women, we honor God. When we live righteously and according to God's commandments, He blesses us in ways that we cannot fully understand.

Do you seek God's peace and His blessings? Then obey Him. When you're faced with a difficult choice or a powerful temptation, seek God's counsel and trust the counsel He gives. Invite God into your heart and live according to His commandments. When you do, you will be blessed today, and tomorrow, and forever.

More Great Ideas About Obedience

Let us never suppose that obedience is impossible or that holiness is meant only for a select few. Our Shepherd leads us in paths of righteousness—not for our name's sake but for His.

Elisabeth Elliot

We cannot rely on God's promises without obeying his commandments.

John Calvin

God uses ordinary people who are obedient to Him to do extraordinary things.

John Maxwell

Believe and do what God says. The life-changing consequences will be limitless, and the results will be confidence and peace of mind.

Franklin Graham

More from God's Word

Who is wise and understanding among you? He should show his works by good conduct with wisdom's gentleness.

James 3:13 HCSB

I have sought You with all my heart; don't let me wander from Your commands.

Psalm 119:10 HCSB

Therefore, everyone who hears these words of Mine and acts on them will be like a sensible man who built his house on the rock. The rain fell, the rivers rose, and the winds blew and pounded that house. Yet it didn't collapse, because its foundation was on the rock.

Matthew 7:24–25 HCSB

Just then someone came up and asked Him, "Teacher, what good must I do to have eternal life?" "Why do you ask Me about what is good?" He said to him. "There is only One who is good. If you want to enter into life, keep the commandments."

Matthew 19:16-17 HCSB

Jesus answered, "If anyone loves Me, he will keep My word. My Father will love him, and We will come to him and make Our home with him."

John 14:23 HCSB

All Scripture is given by inspiration of God, and is profitable for doctrine, for reproof, for correction, for instruction in righteousness, that the man of God may be complete, thoroughly equipped for every good work.

2 Timothy 3:16-17 NKJV

The Use of Scripture

Is Bible study a high priority for you? The answer to this simple question will determine, to a surprising extent, the quality of your life and the direction of your faith.

As you establish priorities for life, you must decide whether God's Word will be a bright spotlight that guides your path every day or a tiny nightlight that occasionally flickers in the dark. The decision to study the Bible—or not—is yours and yours alone. But make no mistake: how you choose to use your Bible will have a profound impact on you and your loved ones.

George Mueller observed, "The vigor of our spiritual lives will be in exact proportion to the place held by the Bible in our lives and in our thoughts." Think of it like this: the more you use your Bible, the more God will use you.

Perhaps you're one of those Christians who owns a bookshelf full of unread Bibles. If so, remember the old saying, "A Bible in the hand is worth two in the bookcase." Or perhaps you're one of those folks who is simply "too busy" to find time for a daily dose of prayer and Bible study. If so, remember the old adage, "It's hard to stumble when you're on your knees."

God's Word can be a roadmap to a place of righteousness and abundance. Make it your roadmap. God's wisdom can be a light to guide your steps. Claim it as your light today, tomorrow, and every day of your life—and then walk confidently in the footsteps of God's only begotten Son.

Heaven and earth will pass away,
but My words will never pass away.

—

Matthew 24:35 HCSB

More Great Ideas About God's Word

Walking in faith brings you to the Word of God. There you will be healed, cleansed, fed, nurtured, equipped, and matured.

Kay Arthur

It takes calm, thoughtful, prayerful meditation on the Word to extract its deepest nourishment.

Vance Havner

God's voice isn't all that difficult to hear. He sometimes shouts through our pain and whispers to us while we're relaxing on vacation. Occasionally, He sings to us in a song and warns us through the sixty-six books of His written Word. It's right there, ink on paper. Count on it—that book will never lead you astray.

Charles Swindoll

The Scriptures were not given for our information, but for our transformation.

D. L. Moody

Help me, Lord, to be a student of Your Word, that I might be a better servant in Your world.

Jim Gallery

Everyone must be quick to hear, slow to speak, and slow to anger, for man's anger does not accomplish God's righteousness.

James 1:19-20 HCSB

The Futility of Anger

If you're like most people, you know a thing or two (or three) about anger. After all, everybody gets mad occasionally, and you're probably no exception.

Anger is a natural human emotion that is sometimes necessary and appropriate. Even Jesus became angry when confronted with the moneychangers in the temple (Matthew 21). Righteous indignation is an appropriate response to evil, but God does not intend that anger should rule our lives. Far from it.

Temper tantrums are usually unproductive, unattractive, unforgettable, and unnecessary. Perhaps that's why Proverbs 16:32 states that, "Controlling your temper is better than capturing a city" (NCV).

If you've allowed anger to become a regular visitor at your house, you should pray for wisdom, for patience, and for a heart that is so filled with forgiveness that it contains no room for bitterness. God will help you terminate your tantrums if you ask Him—and that's a good thing because anger and peace cannot coexist in the same mind.

If you permit yourself to throw too many tantrums, you will forfeit—at least for now—the peace that might otherwise be yours through Christ. So obey God's Word by turning away from anger today and every day. You'll be glad you did, and so will your family and friends.

More Great Ideas About Anger

Get rid of the poison of built-up anger and the acid of long-term resentment.

Charles Swindoll

Anger's the anaesthetic of the mind.

C. S. Lewis

When you lose your temper . . . you lose.

Criswell Freeman

Anger is the noise of the soul; the unseen irritant of the heart; the relentless invader of silence.

Max Lucado

More from God's Word

All bitterness, anger and wrath, insult and slander must be removed from you, along with all wickedness. And be kind and compassionate to one another, forgiving one another, just as God also forgave you in Christ.

Ephesians 4:31-32 HCSB

Don't let your spirit rush to be angry, for anger abides in the heart of fools.

Ecclesiastes 7:9 HCSB

A fool's displeasure is known at once, but whoever ignores an insult is sensible.

Proverbs 12:16 HCSB

A gentle answer turns away anger, but a harsh word stirs up wrath.

Proverbs 15:1 HCSB

But now you must also put away all the following: anger, wrath, malice, slander, and filthy language from your mouth.

Colossians 3:8 HCSB

You shall have no other gods before Me.

Exodus 20:3 NKJV

Putting God First

I
s God your top priority? Have you given His Son your heart, your soul, your talents, and your time? Or are you in the habit of giving God little more than a few hours on Sunday morning? The answers to these questions will determine how you prioritize your days and your life.

As you contemplate your own relationship with God, remember this: all of mankind is engaged in the practice of worship. Some people choose to worship God and, as a result, reap the joy that He intends for His children. Others distance themselves from God by worshiping such things as earthly possessions or personal gratification . . . and when they do so, they suffer.

In the book of Exodus, God warns that we should place no gods before Him. Yet all too often, we place our Lord in second, third, or fourth place as we worship the gods of pride, greed, power, or lust.

When we place our desires for material possessions above our love for God—or when we yield to temptations of the flesh—we find ourselves engaged in a struggle that is similar to the one Jesus faced when He was tempted by Satan. In the wilderness, Satan offered Jesus earthly power and unimaginable riches, but Jesus turned Satan away and chose instead to worship God. We must do likewise by putting God first and worshiping only Him.

Does God rule your heart? Make certain that the honest answer to this question is a resounding yes. In the life of every righteous believer, God comes first. That's precisely the place that He deserves in your heart, too.

Love the Lord your God with
all your heart, with all your soul,
and with all your strength.

—

Deuteronomy 6:5 HCSB

More Great Ideas About Putting God First

A man's spiritual health is exactly proportional to his love for God.

C. S. Lewis

You must never sacrifice your relationship with God for the sake of a relationship with another person.

Charles Stanley

Make God's will the focus of your life day by day. If you seek to please Him and Him alone, you'll find yourself satisfied with life.

Kay Arthur

It is impossible to please God doing things motivated by and produced by the flesh.

Bill Bright

Jesus Christ is the first and last, author and finisher, beginning and end, alpha and omega, and by Him all other things hold together. He must be first or nothing. God never comes next!

Vance Havner

But Jesus turned and saw her. "Have courage, daughter,"
He said. "Your faith has made you well." And the woman
was made well from that moment.

Matthew 9:22 HCSB

His Healing Power

Are you concerned about your spiritual, physical, or emotional health? And would you like to improve these three areas of your life? If so, there is a timeless source of comfort and assurance that is as near as your bookshelf. That source is the Holy Bible.

God's Word has much to say about every aspect of your life, including your health. And, when you face concerns of any sort—including health-related challenges—God is with you. So trust your medical doctor to do his or her part, but place your ultimate trust in your benevolent Heavenly Father.

Talk to God about your health, seek His guidance, and ask Him for the things you need. When you do, He will hear your prayers, and that's a very good thing because His healing touch, like His love, endures forever.

More Great Ideas About Healing

Ultimate healing and the glorification of the body are certainly among the blessings of Calvary for the believing Christian. Immediate healing is not guaranteed.

Warren Wiersbe

The key to healthy eating is moderation and managing what you eat every day.

John Maxwell

You can't buy good health at the doctor's office—you've got to earn it for yourself.

Marie T. Freeman

People are funny. When they are young, they will spend their health to get wealth. Later, they will gladly pay all they have trying to get their health back.

John Maxwell

A Christian should no more defile his body than a Jew would defile the temple.

Warren Wiersbe

The fear of the Lord is the beginning of wisdom, and the knowledge of the Holy One is understanding.

Proverbs 9:10 HCSB

The Right Kind of Fear

Do you have a healthy, fearful respect for God's power? If so, you are both wise and obedient. And, because you are a thoughtful believer, you also understand that genuine wisdom begins with a profound appreciation for God's limitless power.

God praises humility and punishes pride. That's why God's greatest servants will always be those humble men and women who care less for their own glory and more for God's glory. In God's kingdom, the only way to achieve greatness is to shun it. And the only way to be wise is to understand these facts: God is great; He is all-knowing; and He is all-powerful. We must respect Him, and we must humbly obey His commandments, or we must accept the consequences of our misplaced pride.

More Great Ideas About Fearing God

The remarkable thing about fearing God is that when you fear God, you fear nothing else, whereas if you do not fear God, you fear everything else.

Oswald Chambers

If we do not tremble before God, the world's system seems wonderful to us and pleasantly consumes us.

James Montgomery Boice

A healthy fear of God will do much to deter us from sin.

Charles Swindoll

It is not possible that mortal men should be thoroughly conscious of the divine presence without being filled with awe.

C. H. Spurgeon

When true believers are awed by the greatness of God and by the privilege of becoming His children, then they become sincerely motivated, effective evangelists.

Bill Hybels

More from God's Word

The fear of the Lord is the beginning of wisdom; all who follow His instructions have good insight.

Psalm 111:10 HCSB

The fear of the Lord is a fountain of life, turning people from the snares of death.

Proverbs 14:27 HCSB

Don't consider yourself to be wise; fear the Lord and turn away from evil.

Proverbs 3:7 HCSB

The fear of the Lord is the beginning of knowledge, but fools despise wisdom and instruction.

Proverbs 1:7 NKJV

To fear the Lord is to hate evil.

Proverbs 8:13 HCSB

He awakens Me morning by morning, He awakens My ear
to hear as the learned. The Lord God has opened My ear.

Isaiah 50:4-5 NKJV

How to Start the Day

Each new day is a gift from God, and if we are wise, we spend a few quiet moments each morning thanking the Giver. Daily life is woven together with the threads of habit, and no habit is more important to our spiritual health than the discipline of daily prayer and devotion to the Creator.

When we begin each day with heads bowed and hearts lifted, we remind ourselves of God's love, His protection, and His commandments. And if we are wise, we align our priorities for the coming day with the teachings and commandments that God has given us through His Holy Word.

Are you seeking to change some aspect of your life? Do you seek to improve the condition of your spiritual or physical health? If so, ask for God's help and ask for it many times each day . . . starting with your morning devotional.

More Great Ideas About Devotionals

We must appropriate the tender mercy of God every day after conversion or problems quickly develop. We need his grace daily in order to live a righteous life.

Jim Cymbala

Our devotion to God is strengthened when we offer Him a fresh commitment each day.

Elizabeth George

How motivating it has been for me to view my early morning devotions as time of retreat alone with Jesus, Who desires that I "come with Him by myself to a quiet place" in order to pray, read His Word, listen for His voice, and be renewed in my spirit.

Anne Graham Lotz

Think of this—we may live together with Him here and now, a daily walking with Him who loved us and gave Himself for us.

Elisabeth Elliot

I believe the reason so many are failing today is that they have not disciplined themselves to read God's Word consistently, day in and day out, and to apply it to every situation in life.

Kay Arthur

More from God's Word

Lord, You are my lamp; the Lord illuminates my darkness.

2 Samuel 22:29 HCSB

Teach me Your way, Lord, and I will live by Your truth. Give me an undivided mind to fear Your name.

Psalm 86:11 HCSB

I will instruct you and show you the way to go; with My eye on you, I will give counsel.

Psalm 32:8 HCSB

Happy is the man who finds wisdom, and the man who gains understanding.

Proverbs 3:13 NKJV

But grow in the grace and knowledge of our Lord and Savior Jesus Christ. To Him be the glory both now and to the day of eternity.

2 Peter 3:18 HCSB

For if you forgive people their wrongdoing, your heavenly Father will forgive you as well. But if you don't forgive people, your Father will not forgive your wrongdoing.

Matthew 6:14-15 HCSB

Forgiveness Now

Forgiving other people is hard—sometimes very hard. But God tells us that we must forgive others, even when we'd rather not. So, if you're angry with anybody (or if you're upset by something you yourself have done) it's time to forgive . . . now!

Life would be much simpler if you could forgive people "once and for all" and be done with it. Yet forgiveness is seldom that easy. Usually, the decision to forgive is straightforward, but the process of forgiving is more difficult. Forgiveness is a journey that requires effort, time, perseverance, and prayer.

God instructs you to treat other people exactly as you wish to be treated. And since you want to be forgiven for the mistakes that you make, you must be willing to extend forgiveness to other people for the mistakes that they have made. If you can't seem to forgive someone, you should keep asking God to help you until you do. And you can be sure of this: if you keep asking for God's help, He will give it.

More Great Ideas About Forgiveness

Our forgiveness toward others should flow from a realization and appreciation of God's forgiveness toward us.

Franklin Graham

To hold on to hate and resentments is to throw a monkey wrench into the machinery of life.

E. Stanley Jones

I firmly believe a great many prayers are not answered because we are not willing to forgive someone.

D. L. Moody

It is better to forgive and forget than to resent and remember.

Barbara Johnson

As you have received the mercy of God by the forgiveness of sin and the promise of eternal life, thus you must show mercy.

Billy Graham

Whoever believes that Jesus is the Christ is born of God, and everyone who loves Him who begot also loves him who is begotten of Him.

1 John 5:1 NKJV

Give Him Your Heart

Your decision to allow Christ to reign over your heart is the pivotal decision of your life. It is a decision that you cannot ignore. It is a decision that is yours and yours alone.

God's love for you is deeper and more profound than you can imagine. God's love for you is so great that He sent His only Son to this earth to die for your sins and to offer you the priceless gift of eternal life. Now, you must decide whether or not to accept God's gift. Will you ignore it or embrace it? Will you return it or neglect it? Will you accept Christ's love and build a lifelong relationship with Him, or will you turn away from Him and take a different path?

Accept God's gift now: allow His Son to preside over your heart, your thoughts, and your life, starting this very instant.

More Great Ideas About Accepting Christ

It's your heart that Jesus longs for: your will to be made His own with self on the cross forever, and Jesus alone on the throne.

Ruth Bell Graham

The amount of power you experience to live a victorious, triumphant Christian life is directly proportional to the freedom you give the Spirit to be Lord of your life!

Anne Graham Lotz

Choose Jesus Christ! Deny yourself, take up the Cross, and follow Him—for the world must be shown. The world must see, in us, a discernible, visible, startling difference.

Elisabeth Elliot

The most profound essence of my nature is that I am capable of receiving God.

St. Augustine

A man can accept what Christ has done without knowing how it works; indeed, he certainly won't know how it works until he's accepted it.

C. S. Lewis

More from God's Word

For God so loved the world that He gave His only begotten Son, that whoever believes in Him should not perish but have everlasting life.

John 3:16 NKJV

Yet we know that no one is justified by the works of the law but by faith in Jesus Christ. And we have believed in Christ Jesus, so that we might be justified by faith in Christ and not by the works of the law, because by the works of the law no human being will be justified.

Galatians 2:16 HCSB

God wanted to make known to those among the Gentiles the glorious wealth of this mystery, which is Christ in you, the hope of glory.

Colossians 1:27 HCSB

And we have seen and testify that the Father has sent the Son as Savior of the world.

1 John 4:14 NKJV

The Spirit of God, who raised Jesus from the dead, lives in you. And just as he raised Christ from the dead, he will give life to your mortal body by this same Spirit living within you.

Romans 8:11 NLT

Be anxious for nothing, but in everything by prayer and supplication, with thanksgiving, let your requests be made known to God.

Philippians 4:6 NKJV

Beyond Anxiety

We live in a world that often breeds anxiety and fear. When we come face to face with tough times, we may fall prey to discouragement, doubt, or depression. But our Father in Heaven has other plans. God has promised that we may lead lives of abundance, not anxiety. In fact, His Word instructs us to "be anxious for nothing." But how can we put our fears to rest? By taking those fears to God and leaving them there.

As you face the challenges of everyday living, do you find yourself becoming anxious, troubled, discouraged, or fearful? If so, turn every one of your concerns over to your Heavenly Father. The same God who created the universe will comfort you if you ask Him...so ask Him and trust Him. And then watch in amazement as your anxieties melt into the warmth of His loving hands.

More Great Ideas About Anxiety

Some people feel guilty about their anxieties and regard them as a defect of faith, but they are afflictions, not sins. Like all afflictions, they are, if we can so take them, our share in the passion of Christ.

C. S. Lewis

So often we pray and then fret anxiously, waiting for God to hurry up and do something. All the while God is waiting for us to calm down, so He can do something through us.

Corrie ten Boom

Worry and anxiety are sand in the machinery of life; faith is the oil.

E. Stanley Jones

We must lay our questions, frustrations, anxieties, and impotence at the feet of God and wait for His answer. And then receiving it, we must live by faith.

Kay Arthur

The fierce grip of panic need not immobilize you. God knows no limitation when it comes to deliverance. Admit your fear. Commit it to Him. Dump the pressure on Him. He can handle it.

Charles Swindoll

More from God's Word

Therefore don't worry about tomorrow, because tomorrow will worry about itself. Each day has enough trouble of its own.

Matthew 6:34 HCSB

Anxiety in a man's heart weighs it down, but a good word cheers it up.

Proverbs 12:25 HCSB

Why am I so depressed? Why this turmoil within me? Put your hope in God, for I will still praise Him, my Savior and my God.

Psalm 42:11 HCSB

In the multitude of my anxieties within me, Your comforts delight my soul.

Psalm 94:19 NKJV

Let not your heart be troubled: ye believe in God, believe also in me.

John 14:1 KJV

Don't be deceived: God is not mocked. For whatever a man sows he will also reap, because the one who sows to his flesh will reap corruption from the flesh, but the one who sows to the Spirit will reap eternal life from the Spirit.

Galatians 6:7-8 HCSB

Choose Wisely

L ife is a series of choices. Each day, we make countless decisions that can bring us closer to God… or not. When we live according to God's commandments, we earn for ourselves the abundance and peace that He intends for our lives. But, when we turn our backs upon God by disobeying Him, we bring needless suffering upon ourselves and our families.

Do you seek God's peace and His blessings? Then obey Him. When you're faced with a difficult choice or a powerful temptation, seek God's counsel and trust the counsel He gives. Invite God into your heart and live according to His commandments. When you do, you will be blessed today, and tomorrow, and forever.

More Great Ideas About Behavior

Live in such a way that any day would make a suitable capstone for life. Live so that you need not change your mode of living, even if your sudden departure were immediately predicted to you.

C. H. Spurgeon

Don't worry about what you do not understand. Worry about what you do understand in the Bible but do not live by.

Corrie ten Boom

More depends on my walk than my talk.

D. L. Moody

Our response to God determines His response to us.

Henry Blackaby

There may be no trumpet sound or loud applause when we make a right decision, just a calm sense of resolution and peace.

Gloria Gaither

More from God's Word

Therefore, get your minds ready for action, being self-disciplined, and set your hope completely on the grace to be brought to you at the revelation of Jesus Christ. As obedient children, do not be conformed to the desires of your former ignorance but, as the One who called you is holy, you also are to be holy in all your conduct.

1 Peter 1:13-15 HCSB

Lead a tranquil and quiet life in all godliness and dignity.

1 Timothy 2:2 HCSB

For this very reason, make every effort to supplement your faith with goodness, goodness with knowledge, knowledge with self-control, self-control with endurance, endurance with godliness.

2 Peter 1:5-6 HCSB

Therefore as you have received Christ Jesus the Lord, walk in Him.

Colossians 2:6 HCSB

He will teach us of his ways, and we will walk in his paths.

Isaiah 2:3 KJV

Then He said to Thomas, "Put your finger here and observe My hands. Reach out your hand and put it into My side. Don't be an unbeliever, but a believer."

John 20:27 HCSB

Actions and Beliefs

Our theology must be demonstrated, not only by our words but, more importantly, by our actions. As Christians, we must do our best to make sure that our actions are accurate reflections of our beliefs. In short, we should be practical believers, quick to act whenever we see an opportunity to serve God.

We may proclaim our beliefs to our hearts' content, but our proclamations will mean nothing—to others or to ourselves—unless we accompany our words with deeds that match. The sermons that we live are far more compelling than the ones we preach. So remember this: whether you like it or not, your life is an accurate reflection of your creed. If this fact gives you cause for concern, don't bother talking about the changes that you intend to make—make them. And then, when your good deeds speak for themselves—as they most certainly will—don't interrupt.

More Great Ideas About Belief

What we believe determines how we behave, and both determine what we become.

Warren Wiersbe

What I believe about God is the most important thing about me.

A. W. Tozer

The reason many of us do not ardently believe in the gospel is that we have never given it a rigorous testing, thrown our hard questions at it, or faced it with our most prickly doubts.

Eugene Peterson

I believe in Christ as I believe in that the Sun has risen, not only because I see it, but because by it I see everything else.

C. S. Lewis

God delights to meet the faith of one who looks up to Him and says, "Lord, You know that I cannot do this— but I believe that You can!"

Amy Carmichael

More from God's Word

Everyone who believes that Jesus is the Messiah has been born of God, and everyone who loves the parent also loves his child.

1 John 5:1 HCSB

I know whom I have believed and am persuaded that He is able to guard what has been entrusted to me until that day.

2 Timothy 1:12 HCSB

Then Jesus told the centurion, "Go. As you have believed, let it be done for you." And his servant was cured that very moment.

Matthew 8:13 HCSB

Blessed are those who hunger and thirst for righteousness, For they shall be filled.

Matthew 5:6 NKJV

The Lord bless you and keep you; the Lord make His face shine upon you, and be gracious to you.

Numbers 6:24-25 NKJV

Counting Your Blessings

If you sat down and began counting your blessings, how long would it take? A very, very long time! Your blessings include life, freedom, family, friends, talents, and possessions, for starters. But, your greatest blessing—a gift that is yours for the asking—is God's gift of salvation through Christ Jesus.

Today, begin making a list of your blessings. You most certainly will not be able to make a complete list, but take a few moments and jot down as many blessings as you can. Then give thanks to the giver of all good things: God. His love for you is eternal, as are His gifts. And it's never too soon—or too late—to offer Him thanks.

I will make them and the area around My hill a blessing: I will send down showers in their season— showers of blessing.

—

Ezekiel 34:26 HCSB

More Great Ideas About Blessings

Jesus intended for us to be overwhelmed by the blessings of regular days. He said it was the reason he had come: "I am come that they might have life, and that they might have it more abundantly."

Gloria Gaither

God's kindness is not like the sunset—brilliant in its intensity, but dying every second. God's generosity keeps coming and coming and coming.

Bill Hybels

When you and I are related to Jesus Christ, our strength and wisdom and peace and joy and love and hope may run out, but His life rushes in to keep us filled to the brim. We are showered with blessings, not because of anything we have or have not done, but simply because of Him.

Anne Graham Lotz

Do we not continually pass by blessings innumerable without notice, and instead fix our eyes on what we feel to be our trials and our losses, and think and talk about these until our whole horizon is filled with them, and we almost begin to think we have no blessings at all?

Hannah Whitall Smith

I the Lord do not change.

Malachi 3:6 HCSB

What Doesn't Change

We live in a world that is always changing, but we worship the God who never changes—thank goodness! That means that we can be comforted in the knowledge that our Heavenly Father is the rock that simply cannot be moved.

The next time you face difficult circumstances, tough times, unfair treatment, or unwelcome changes, remember that some things never change—things like the love that you feel in your heart for your family and friends . . . and the love that God feels for you. So, instead of worrying too much about life's inevitable challenges, focus your energies on finding solutions. Have faith in your own abilities, do your best to solve your problems, and leave the rest up to God.

Create in me a clean heart, O God,
and renew a steadfast spirit within me.

—

Psalm 51:10 NKJV

More Great Ideas About Change

The fewer words, the better prayer.

Martin Luther

Part of good communication is listening with the eyes as well as with the ears.

Josh McDowell

How much of our lives are, well, so daily. How often our hours are filled with the mundane, seemingly unimportant things that have to be done, whether at home or work. These very "daily" tasks could become a celebration of praise. "It is through consecration," someone has said, "that drudgery is made divine."

Gigi Graham Tchividjian

Some of us seem so anxious about avoiding hell that we forget to celebrate our journey toward heaven.

Philip Yancey

God has a course mapped out for your life, and all the inadequacies in the world will not change His mind. He will be with you every step of the way. And though it may take time, He has a celebration planned for when you cross over the "Red Seas" of your life.

Charles Swindoll

The man of integrity walks securely, but he who takes crooked paths will be found out.

Proverbs 10:9 NIV

Character Counts

It has been said that character is what we are when nobody is watching. How true. If we sincerely wish to walk with God, we must strive, to the best of our abilities, to follow God's path and to obey His instructions. In short, we must recognize the importance that integrity should play in our lives.

When we listen carefully to the conscience that God has placed within our hearts, and when we behave in ways that are consistent with our beliefs, we can't help but to receive God's blessings.

So today and every day, give yourself a gift by listening carefully to your conscience. Build your life on the firm foundation of integrity. When you do, you won't need to look over your shoulder to see who, besides God, is watching.

More Great Ideas About Character

Maintaining your integrity in a world of sham is no small accomplishment.

Wayne Oates

Image is what people think we are; integrity is what we really are.

John Maxwell

The trials of life can be God's tools for engraving His image on our character.

Warren Wiersbe

There is no way to grow a saint overnight. Character, like the oak tree, does not spring up like a mushroom.

Vance Havner

In matters of style, swim with the current. In matters of principle, stand like a rock.

Thomas Jefferson

More from God's Word

We also rejoice in our afflictions, because we know that affliction produces endurance, endurance produces proven character, and proven character produces hope.

Romans 5:3-4 HCSB

As for you, if you walk before Me as your father David walked, with integrity of heart and uprightness, doing everything I have commanded you, and if you keep My statutes and ordinances, I will establish your royal throne over Israel forever, as I promised your father David.

1 Kings 9:4-5 HCSB

The righteousness of the blameless clears his path, but the wicked person will fall because of his wickedness.

Proverbs 11:5 HCSB

A good name is to be chosen over great wealth.

Proverbs 22:1 HCSB

As the water reflects the face, so the heart reflects the person.

Proverbs 27:19 HCSB

A merry heart does good, like medicine.

Proverbs 17:22 NKJV

Cheerfulness Is a Gift

Cheerfulness is a gift that we give to others and to ourselves. And, as believers who have been saved by a risen Christ, why shouldn't we be cheerful? The answer, of course, is that we have every reason to honor our Savior with joy in our hearts, smiles on our faces, and words of celebration on our lips.

Few things in life are more sad, or, for that matter, more absurd, than grumpy Christians. Christ promises us lives of abundance and joy if we accept His love and His grace. Yet sometimes, even the most righteous among us are beset by fits of ill temper and frustration. During these moments, we may not feel like turning our thoughts and prayers to Christ, but if we seek to gain perspective and peace, that's precisely what we must do.

Are you a cheerful Christian? You should be! And what is the best way to attain the joy that is rightfully yours? By giving Christ what is rightfully His: your heart, your soul, and your life.

More Great Ideas About Cheerfulness

The people whom I have seen succeed best in life have always been cheerful and hopeful people who went about their business with a smile on their faces.

Charles Kingsley

God is good, and heaven is forever. And if those two facts don't cheer you up, nothing will.

Marie T. Freeman

Sour godliness is the devil's religion.

John Wesley

We may run, walk, stumble, drive, or fly, but let us never lose sight of the reason for the journey, or miss a chance to see a rainbow on the way.

Gloria Gaither

Christ can put a spring in your step and a thrill in your heart. Optimism and cheerfulness are products of knowing Christ.

Billy Graham

I have learned to be content in whatever circumstances I am.

Philippians 4:11 HCSB

Finding Contentment

The preoccupation with happiness and contentment is an ever-present theme in the modern world. We are bombarded with messages that tell us where to find peace and pleasure in a world that worships materialism and wealth. But, lasting contentment is not found in material possessions; genuine contentment is a spiritual gift from God to those who trust in Him and follow His commandments.

Where do we find contentment? If we don't find it in God, we will never find it anywhere else. But, if we put our faith and our trust in Him, we will be blessed with an inner peace that is beyond human understanding. When God dwells at the center of our lives, peace and contentment will belong to us just as surely as we belong to God.

More Great Ideas About Contentment

God would rather have a man on the wrong side of the fence than on the fence. The worst enemies of apostles are not the opposers but the appeasers.

Vance Havner

God is able to do anything He pleases with one ordinary person fully consecrated to Him.

Henry Blackaby and Claude King

We become whatever we are committed to.

Rick Warren

Commitment doesn't come easy, but when you're fighting for something you believe in, the struggle is worth it.

John Maxwell

When we give ourselves wholly to God, He takes from our meager reserves and gives back from infinity. What a marvelous exchange!

Shirley Dobson

More from God's Word

A tranquil heart is life to the body, but jealousy is rottenness to the bones.

Proverbs 14:30 HCSB

The LORD will give strength to His people; the LORD will bless His people with peace.

Psalm 29:11 NKJV

Let your conduct be without covetousness; be content with such things as you have. For He Himself has said, "I will never leave you nor forsake you."

Hebrews 13:5 NKJV

But godliness with contentment is a great gain. For we brought nothing into the world, and we can take nothing out. But if we have food and clothing, we will be content with these. But those who want to be rich fall into temptation, a trap, and many foolish and harmful desires, which plunge people into ruin and destruction.

1 Timothy 6:6-9 HCSB

Be strong and courageous, and do the work. Don't be afraid or discouraged, for the Lord God, my God, is with you. He won't leave you or forsake you.

1 Chronicles 28:20 HCSB

Courage for Today

Christians have every reason to live courageously. After all, the ultimate battle has already been won on the cross at Calvary. But even dedicated followers of Christ may find their courage tested by the inevitable disappointments and fears that visit the lives of believers and non-believers alike.

When you find yourself worried about the challenges of today or the uncertainties of tomorrow, you must ask yourself whether or not you are ready to place your concerns and your life in God's all-powerful, all-knowing, all-loving hands. If the answer to that question is yes—as it should be—then you can draw courage today from the source of strength that never fails: your Heavenly Father.

More Great Ideas About Courage

With each new experience of letting God be in control, we gain courage and reinforcement for daring to do it again and again.

Gloria Gaither

When once we are assured that God is good, then there can be nothing left to fear.

Hannah Whitall Smith

Are you fearful? First, bow your head and pray for God's strength. Then, raise your head knowing that, together, you and God can handle whatever comes your way.

Jim Gallery

There comes a time when we simply have to face the challenges in our lives and stop backing down.

John Eldredge

The truth of Christ brings assurance and so removes the former problem of fear and uncertainty.

A. W. Tozer

More from God's Word

For God has not given us a spirit of fearfulness, but one of power, love, and sound judgment.

2 Timothy 1:7 HCSB

Be alert, stand firm in the faith, be brave and strong.

1 Corinthians 16:13 HCSB

Haven't I commanded you: be strong and courageous? Do not be afraid or discouraged, for the Lord your God is with you wherever you go.

Joshua 1:9 HCSB

But when Jesus heard it, He answered him, "Don't be afraid. Only believe."

Luke 8:50 HCSB

But He said to them, "Why are you fearful, you of little faith?" Then He got up and rebuked the winds and the sea. And there was a great calm.

Matthew 8:26 HCSB

Therefore, if anyone is in Christ, he is a new creation; old things have passed away; behold, all things have become new.

2 Corinthians 5:17 NKJV

The New You

In 2 Corinthians 5:17, we are told that when a person accepts Christ, he or she becomes a new creation. Have you invited God's Son to reign over your heart and your life? If so, think for a moment about the "old" you, the person you were before you invited Christ into your heart. Now, think about the "new" you, the person you have become since then. Is there a difference between the "old" you and the "new and improved" version? There should be! And that difference should be noticeable not only to you but also to others.

Warren Wiersbe observed, "The greatest miracle of all is the transformation of a lost sinner into a child of God." And Oswald Chambers noted, "If the Spirit of God has transformed you within, you will exhibit Divine characteristics in your life, not good human characteristics. God's life in us expresses itself as God's life, not as a human life trying to be godly."

When you invited Christ to reign over your heart, you became a new creation through Him. This day offers yet another opportunity to behave yourself like that new creation by serving your Creator and strengthening your character. When you do, God will guide your steps and bless your endeavors today and forever.

More Great Ideas About Conversion

Being born again is God's solution to our need for love and life and light.

Anne Graham Lotz

Before God changes our circumstances, He wants to change our hearts.

Warren Wiersbe

No one can be converted except with the consent of his own free will because God does not override human choice.

Billy Graham

We had better quickly discover whether we have mere religion or a real experience with Jesus, whether we have outward observance of religious forms or hearts that beat in tune with God.

Jim Cymbala

More from God's Word

Jesus replied, "I assure you: Unless someone is born again, he cannot see the kingdom of God." "But how can anyone be born when he is old?" Nicodemus asked Him. "Can he enter his mother's womb a second time and be born?" Jesus answered, "I assure you: Unless someone is born of water and the Spirit, he cannot enter the kingdom of God."

John 3:3–5 HCSB

Then He called a child to Him and had him stand among them. "I assure you," He said, "unless you are converted and become like children, you will never enter the kingdom of heaven."

Matthew 18:2-3 HCSB

Therefore we were buried with Him by baptism into death, in order that, just as Christ was raised from the dead by the glory of the Father, so we too may walk in a new way of life.

Romans 6:4 HCSB

Everyone who believes that Jesus is the Messiah has been born of God, and everyone who loves the parent also loves his child.

1 John 5:1 HCSB

But Jesus looked at them and said to them, "With men this is impossible, but with God all things are possible."

Matthew 19:26 NKJV

With God, All Things Are Possible

Sometimes, because we are imperfect human beings with limited understanding and limited faith, we place limitations on God. But, God's power has no limitations. God will work miracles in our lives if we trust Him with everything we have and everything we are. When we do, we experience the miraculous results of His endless love and His awesome power.

Miracles, both great and small, are an integral part of everyday life, but usually, we are too busy or too cynical to notice God's handiwork. We don't expect to see miracles, so we simply overlook them.

Do you lack the faith that God can work miracles in your own life? If so, it's time to reconsider. If you have allowed yourself to become a "doubting Thomas," you are attempting to place limitations on a God who has none. Instead of doubting God, you must trust Him. Then, you must wait and watch because something miraculous is going to happen to you, and it might just happen today.

More Great Ideas About Miracles

Are you looking for a miracle? If you keep your eyes wide open and trust in God, you won't have to look very far.

Marie T. Freeman

The miracles in fact are a retelling in small letters of the very same story which is written across the whole world in letters too large for some of us to see.

C. S. Lewis

We have a God who delights in impossibilities.

Andrew Murray

Never be afraid to hope—or to ask—for a miracle.

Criswell Freeman

I have been suspected of being what is called a fundamentalist. That is because I never regard any narrative as unhistorical simply on the ground that it includes the miraculous.

C. S. Lewis

More from God's Word

Is anything impossible for the Lord?

Genesis 18:14 HCSB

But as it is written: "Eye has not seen, nor ear heard, nor have entered into the heart of man the things which God has prepared for those who love Him."

1 Corinthians 2:9 NKJV

I assure you: The one who believes in Me will also do the works that I do. And he will do even greater works than these, because I am going to the Father.

John 14:12 HCSB

Looking at them, Jesus said, "With men it is impossible, but not with God, because all things are possible with God."

Mark 10:27 HCSB

You are the God who works wonders; You revealed Your strength among the peoples.

Psalm 77:14 HCSB

Make a joyful noise unto the LORD, all ye lands. Serve the LORD with gladness: come before his presence with singing.

Psalm 100:1-2 KJV

Make a Joyful Noise

When is the best time to "make a joyful noise" by praising God? In church? Before dinner is served? When we tuck little children into bed? None of the above. The best time to praise God is all day, every day, to the greatest extent we can, with thanksgiving in our hearts, and with a song on our lips.

Too many of us, even well-intentioned believers, tend to compartmentalize our waking hours into a few familiar categories: work, rest, play, family time, and worship. To do so is a mistake. Worship and praise should be woven into the fabric of everything we do; it should never be relegated to a weekly three-hour visit to church on Sunday morning.

Theologian Wayne Oates once admitted, "Many of my prayers are made with my eyes open. You see, it seems I'm always praying about something, and it's not always convenient—or safe—to close my eyes." Dr. Oates understood that God always hears our prayers and that the relative position of our eyelids is of no concern to Him.

Today, find a little more time to lift your concerns to God in prayer, and praise Him for all that He has done. Whether your eyes are open or closed, He's listening.

More Great Ideas About Joy

Where the soul is full of peace and joy, outward surroundings and circumstances are of comparatively little account.

Hannah Whitall Smiith

Gratitude changes the pangs of memory into a tranquil joy.

Dietrich Bonhoeffer

As Catherine of Siena said, "All the way to heaven is heaven." A joyful end requires a joyful means. Bless the Lord.

Eugene Peterson

He wants us to have a faith that does not complain while waiting, but rejoices because we know our times are in His hands—nail-scarred hands that labor for our highest good.

Kay Arthur

More from God's Word

Thou wilt show me the path of life: in thy presence is fulness of joy; at thy right hand there are pleasures for evermore.

Psalm 16:11 KJV

Praise the Lord, all nations! Glorify Him, all peoples! For great is His faithful love to us; the Lord's faithfulness endures forever. Hallelujah!

Psalm 117 HCSB

But I will hope continually and will praise You more and more.

Psalm 71:14 HCSB

Therefore, through Him let us continually offer up to God a sacrifice of praise, that is, the fruit of our lips that confess His name.

Hebrews 13:15 HCSB

So that at the name of Jesus every knee should bow—of those who are in heaven and on earth and under the earth—and every tongue should confess that Jesus Christ is Lord, to the glory of God the Father.

Philippians 2:10-11 HCSB

To everything there is a season, a time for every purpose under heaven

Ecclesiastes 3:1 NKJV

Trust God's Timing

Sometimes, the hardest thing to do is to wait. This is especially true when we're in a hurry and when we want things to happen now, if not sooner! But God's plan does not always happen in the way that we would like or at the time of our own choosing. Our task—as thoughtful men and women who trust in a benevolent, all-knowing Father—is to wait patiently for God to reveal Himself.

We humans know precisely what we want, and we know exactly when we want it. But, God has a far better plan for each of us. He has created a world that unfolds according to His own timetable, not ours . . . thank goodness! And if we're wise, we trust Him and we wait patiently for Him. After all, He is trustworthy, and He always knows best.

More Great Ideas About God's Timing

He makes us wait. He keeps us in the dark on purpose. He makes us walk when we want to run, sit still when we want to walk, for He has things to do in our souls that we are not interested in.

Elisabeth Elliot

The stops of a good man are ordered by the Lord as well as his steps.

George Mueller

You have a timetable, and God has a timetable. His is better than yours.

Criswell Freeman

Waiting on God brings us to the journey's end quicker than our feet.

Mrs. Charles E. Cowman

God does not promise to keep us out of the storms and floods, but He does promise to sustain us in the storm, and then bring us out in due time for His glory when the storm has done its work.

Warren Wiersbe

More from God's Word

Therefore the Lord is waiting to show you mercy, and is rising up to show you compassion, for the Lord is a just God. Happy are all who wait patiently for Him.

Isaiah 30:18 HCSB

Wait for the Lord; be courageous and let your heart be strong. Wait for the Lord.

Psalm 27:14 HCSB

He said to them, "It is not for you to know times or periods that the Father has set by His own authority."

Acts 1:7 HCSB

For My thoughts are not your thoughts, and your ways are not My ways. For as heaven is higher than earth, so My ways are higher than your ways, and My thoughts than your thoughts.

Isaiah 55:8-9 HCSB

Can you understand the secrets of God? His limits are higher than the heavens; you cannot reach them! They are deeper than the grave; you cannot understand them! His limits are longer than the earth and wider than the sea.

Job 11:7-9 NCV

Weeping may endure for a night, but joy comes in the morning.

Psalm 30:5 NKJV

Beyond Grief

Grief visits all of us who live long and love deeply. When we lose a loved one, or when we experience any other profound loss, darkness overwhelms us for a while, and it seems as if our purpose for living has vanished. Thankfully, God has other plans.

The Christian faith, as communicated through the words of the Holy Bible, is a healing faith. It offers comfort in times of trouble, courage for our fears, hope instead of hopelessness. For Christians, the grave is not a final resting-place, it is a place of transition. Through the healing words of God's promises, Christians understand that the Lord continues to manifest His plan in good times and bad.

God intends that you have a meaningful, abundant life, but He expects you to do your part in claiming those blessings. So, as you work through your grief, you will find it helpful to utilize all the resources that God has placed along your path. God makes help available, but it's up to you to find it and then to accept it.

If you are experiencing the intense pain of a recent loss, or if you are still mourning a loss from long ago, perhaps you are now ready to begin the next stage of your journey with God. If so, be mindful of this fact: As a wounded survivor, you will have countless opportunities to serve others. And by serving others, you will bring purpose and meaning to the suffering you've endured.

I have heard your prayer;
I have seen your tears.
Look, I will heal you.

—

2 Kings 20:5 HCSB

More Great Ideas About Overcoming Grief

In times of deepest suffering it is the faithful carrying out of ordinary duties that brings the greatest consolation.

Elisabeth Elliot

The grace of God is sufficient for all our needs, for every problem and for every difficulty, for every broken heart, and for every human sorrow.

Peter Marshall

To pray much is to knock for Him to Whom we pray. This is often done more by groans than speeches, by weeping than by addresses.

St. Augustine

He who becomes a brother to the bruised, a doctor to the despairing, and a comforter to the crushed may not actually say much. What he has to offer is often beyond the power of speech to convey. But, the weary sense it, and it is a balm of Gilead to their souls.

Vance Havner

You learn your theology most where your sorrows take you.

Martin Luther

Jesus said to him, "'You shall love the Lord your God with all your heart, with all your soul, and with all your mind.' This is the first and great commandment."

Matthew 22:37-38 NKJV

Loving God

Christ's words are unambiguous: "Love the Lord your God with all your heart and with all your soul and with all your mind." But sometimes, despite our best intentions, we fall short of God's plan for our lives when we become embittered with ourselves, with our neighbors, or most especially with our Creator.

If we are to please God, we must cleanse ourselves of the negative feelings that separate us from others and from Him. In 1 Corinthians 13, we are told that love is the foundation upon which all our relationships are to be built: our relationships with others and our relationship with our Maker.

So today and every day, fill your heart with love; never yield to bitterness; and praise the Son of God who, in His infinite wisdom, made love His greatest commandment.

More Great Ideas About Loving God

Man was created by God to know and love Him in a permanent, personal relationship.

Anne Graham Lotz

Whatever you love most, be it sports, pleasure, business or God, that is your god.

Billy Graham

In true religion, to love God and to know God are synonymous terms.

C. H. Spurgeon

A man's spiritual health is exactly proportional to his love for God.

C. S. Lewis

I love Him because He first loved me, and He still does love me, and He will love me forever and ever.

Bill Bright

More from God's Word

This is how we know that we love God's children when we love God and obey His commands.

1 John 5:2 HCSB

Love the Lord your God with all your heart, with all your soul, and with all your strength. These words that I am giving you today are to be in your heart. Repeat them to your children. Talk about them when you sit in your house and when you walk along the road, when you lie down and when you get up.

Deuteronomy 6:5-7 HCSB

And we know that all things work together for good to them that love God, to them who are the called according to his purpose.

Romans 8:28 KJV

So that at the name of Jesus every knee should bow—of those who are in heaven and on earth and under the earth—and every tongue should confess that Jesus Christ is Lord, to the glory of God the Father.

Philippians 2:10-11 HCSB

Worship the Lord your God and . . . serve Him only.

Matthew 4:10 HCSB

Do not fear, for I am with you; do not be afraid, for I am your God. I will strengthen you; I will help you; I will hold on to you with My righteous right hand.

Isaiah 41:10 HCSB

Above and Beyond Fear

We live in a fear-based world, a world where bad new travels at light speed and good news doesn't. These are troubled times, times when we have legitimate fears for the future of our nation, our world, and our families. But we also have every reason to live courageously. After all, since God has promised to love us and protect us, who—or what—should we fear?

Perhaps you, like countless others, have found your courage tested by the anxieties and fears that are an inevitable part of life. If so, let the words of Isaiah 41:10 serve as a reminder that God wants to you to think less about your challenges and more about His love. Remember that He is not just near, He is here, and He's ready to help right now. God will comfort you if you ask Him to. So why not ask? And why not now?

More Great Ideas About Fear

Our future may look fearfully intimidating, yet we can look up to the Engineer of the Universe, confident that nothing escapes His attention or slips out of the control of those strong hands.

Elisabeth Elliot

Earthly fears are no fears at all. Answer the big question of eternity, and the little questions of life fall into perspective.

Max Lucado

There is not only fear, but terrible danger, for the life unguarded by God.

Oswald Chambers

The Bible is a Christian's guidebook, and I believe the knowledge it sheds on pain and suffering is the great antidote to fear for suffering people. Knowledge can dissolve fear as light destroys darkness.

Philip Yancey

Courage faces fear and thereby masters it. Cowardice represses fear and is thereby mastered by it.

Martin Luther King, Jr.

More from God's Word

Don't be afraid. Only believe.

Mark 5:36 HCSB

Even when I go through the darkest valley, I fear no danger, for You are with me.

Psalm 23:4 HCSB

I sought the Lord, and He heard me, and delivered me from all my fears.

Psalm 34:4 NKJV

Do not fear, for I am with you; do not be afraid, for I am your God. I will strengthen you; I will help you; I will hold on to you with My righteous right hand.

Isaiah 41:10 HCSB

Indeed, God is my salvation. I will trust Him and not be afraid.

Isaiah 12:2 HCSB

The LORD is gracious and full of compassion, slow to anger and great in mercy. The LORD is good to all, and His tender mercies are over all His works.

Psalm 145:8-9 NKJV

God's Mercy

In Psalm 145, we are taught that God is merciful. His hand offers forgiveness and salvation. God's mercy, like His love, is infinite and everlasting—it knows no boundaries.

Romans 3:23 reminds us of a universal truth: "All have sinned, and come short of the glory of God" (KJV). All of us, even the most righteous among us, are sinners. But despite our imperfections, our merciful Father in heaven offers us salvation through the person of His Son.

As Christians, we have been blessed by a merciful, loving God. Now, it's our turn to share His love and His mercy with a world that needs both. May we accept His gifts and share them with our friends, with our families, and with all the people He chooses to place along our paths.

More Great Ideas About God's Mercy

Angels descending, bring from above, echoes of mercy, whispers of love.

Fanny Crosby

We must appropriate the tender mercy of God every day after conversion, or problems quickly develop. We need his grace daily in order to live a righteous life.

Jim Cymbala

The Creator has given to us the awesome responsibility of representing him to our children. Our heavenly Father is a God of unlimited love, and our children must become acquainted with his mercy and tenderness through our own love toward them.

James Dobson

Storm the throne of grace and persevere therein, and mercy will come down.

John Wesley

Mercy is an attribute of God, an infinite and inexhaustible energy within the divine nature which disposes God to be actively compassionate.

A. W. Tozer

More from God's Word

Help me, O Lord my God! Oh, save me according to Your mercy.

Psalm 109:26 NKJV

He has shown you, O man, what is good; and what does the LORD require of you but to do justly, to love mercy, and to walk humbly with your God?

Micah 6:8 NKJV

See, we count as blessed those who have endured. You have heard of Job's endurance and have seen the outcome from the Lord: the Lord is very compassionate and merciful.

James 5:11 HCSB

But God, who is abundant in mercy, because of His great love that He had for us, made us alive with the Messiah even though we were dead in trespasses. By grace you are saved!

Ephesians 2:4-5 HCSB

Therefore let us approach the throne of grace with boldness, so that we may receive mercy and find grace to help us at the proper time.

Hebrews 4:16 HCSB

Guard your heart above all else, for it is the source of life.

Proverbs 4:23 HCSB

Guard Your Heart

You are near and dear to God. He loves you more than you can imagine, and He wants the very best for you. And one more thing: God wants you to guard your heart.

Every day, you are faced with choices . . . more choices than you can count. You can do the right thing, or not. You can be prudent, or not. You can be kind, and generous, and obedient to God. Or not.

Today, the world will offer you countless opportunities to let down your guard and, by doing so, make needless mistakes that may injure you or your loved ones. So be watchful and obedient. Guard your heart by giving it to your Heavenly Father; it is safe with Him.

More Great Ideas About Guarding Your Heart

The more wisdom enters our hearts, the more we will be able to trust our hearts in difficult situations.

John Eldredge

We can't stop the Adversary from whispering in our ears, but we can refuse to listen, and we can definitely refuse to respond.

Liz Curtis Higgs

Our actions are seen by people, but our motives are monitored by God.

Franklin Graham

To lose heart is to lose everything.

John Eldredge

A man's poverty before God is judged by the disposition of his heart, not by his coffers.

St. Augustine

More from God's Word

The peace of God, which surpasses all understanding, will guard your hearts and minds through Christ Jesus.

Philippians 4:7 NKJV

Keep your heart with all diligence, for out of it spring the issues of life. Put away from you a deceitful mouth, and put perverse lips far from you. Let your eyes look straight ahead, and your eyelids look right before you. Ponder the path of your feet, and let all your ways be established. Do not turn to the right or the left; remove your foot from evil.

Proverbs 4:23-27 NKJV

Sow righteousness for yourselves and reap faithful love; break up your untilled ground. It is time to seek the Lord until He comes and sends righteousness on you like the rain.

Hosea 10:12 HCSB

Blessed are the pure in heart, because they will see God.

Matthew 5:8 HCSB

Finally, brethren, whatever things are true, whatever things are noble, whatever things are just, whatever things are pure, whatever things are lovely, whatever things are of good report, if there is any virtue and if there is anything praiseworthy— meditate on these things.

Philippians 4:8 NKJV

Even though I walk through the valley of the shadow of death, I will fear no evil, for you are with me; your rod and your staff, they comfort me.

Psalm 23:4 NIV

Trust the Shepherd

In the 23rd Psalm, David teaches us that God is like a watchful shepherd caring for His flock. No wonder these verses have provided comfort and hope for generations of believers.

You are precious in the eyes of God. You are His priceless creation, made in His image, and protected by Him. God watches over every step you make and every breath you take, so you need never be afraid. But sometimes, fear has a way of slipping into the minds and hearts of even the most devout believers—and you are no exception.

You know from firsthand experience that life is not always easy. But as a recipient of God's grace, you also know that you are protected by a loving Heavenly Father.

On occasion, you will confront circumstances that trouble you to the very core of your soul. When you are afraid, trust in God. When you are worried, turn your concerns over to Him. When you are anxious, be still and listen for the quiet assurance of God's promises. And then, place your life in His hands. He is your Shepherd today and throughout eternity. Trust the Shepherd.

He comforts us in all our affliction, so that we may be able to comfort those who are in any kind of affliction, through the comfort we ourselves receive from God.

—

2 Corinthians 1:4 HCSB

More Great Ideas About God's Comfort

Pour out your heart to God and tell Him how you feel. Be real, be honest, and when you get it all out, you'll start to feel the gradual covering of God's comforting presence.

Bill Hybels

God's promises are medicine for the broken heart. Let Him comfort you. And, after He has comforted you, try to share that comfort with somebody else. It will do both of you good.

Warren Wiersbe

My prayer for you today is that you will feel the loving arms of God wrapped around you.

Billy Graham

To know that God rules over all—that there are no accidents in life, that no tactic of Satan or man can ever thwart the will of God—brings divine comfort.

Kay Arthur

When I am criticized, injured, or afraid, there is a Father who is ready to comfort me.

Max Lucado

More from God's Word

The Lord is gracious and compassionate, slow to anger and great in faithful love. The Lord is good to everyone; His compassion [rests] on all He has made.

Psalm 145:8-9 HCSB

God is faithful, by whom you were called into the fellowship of His Son, Jesus Christ our Lord.

1 Corinthians 1:9 NKJV

Those who trust in the Lord are like Mount Zion. It cannot be shaken; it remains forever.

Psalm 125:1 HCSB

Therefore don't worry about tomorrow, because tomorrow will worry about itself. Each day has enough trouble of its own.

Matthew 6:34 HCSB

I will be with you when you pass through the waters . . . when you walk through the fire . . . the flame will not burn you. For I the Lord your God, the Holy One of Israel, and your Savior.

Isaiah 43:2-3 HCSB

God is our refuge and strength, a very present help in trouble.

Psalm 46:1 NKJV

God Is Our Refuge

The words of Psalm 46:1 promise that God is our refuge, a refuge that we all need. From time to time, all of us face adversity, discouragement, or disappointment. And throughout life, we all must endure life-changing personal losses that leave us breathless. When we do, God stands ready to protect us. Psalm 147 assures us that, "He heals the brokenhearted, and binds their wounds" (v. 3, NIV).

Are you anxious? Take those anxieties to God. Are you troubled? Take your troubles to Him. Does the world seem to be trembling beneath your feet? Seek protection from the One who cannot be moved.

The same God who created the universe stands ready and willing to comfort you and to restore your strength. During life's most difficult days, your Heavenly Father remains steadfast. And, in His own time and according to His master plan, He will heal you if you invite Him into your heart.

More Great Ideas About Tough Times

Even in the winter, even in the midst of the storm, the sun is still there. Somewhere, up above the clouds, it still shines and warms and pulls at the life buried deep inside the brown branches and frozen earth. The sun is there! Spring will come.

Gloria Gaither

God allows us to experience the low points of life in order to teach us lessons that we could learn in no other way.

C. S. Lewis

Our loving God uses difficulty in our lives to burn away the sin of self and build faith and spiritual power.

Bill Bright

Adversity is always unexpected and unwelcomed. It is an intruder and a thief, and yet in the hands of God, adversity becomes the means through which His supernatural power is demonstrated.

Charles Swindoll

The sermon of your life in tough times ministers to people more powerfully than the most eloquent speaker.

Bill Bright

More from God's Word

Consider it a great joy, my brothers, whenever you experience various trials, knowing that the testing of your faith produces endurance. But endurance must do its complete work, so that you may be mature and complete, lacking nothing.

James 1:2-4 HCSB

When you are in distress and all these things have happened to you, you will return to the Lord your God in later days and obey Him. He will not leave you, destroy you, or forget the covenant with your fathers that He swore to them by oath, because the Lord your God is a compassionate God.

Deuteronomy 4:30-31 HCSB

Dear friends, when the fiery ordeal arises among you to test you, don't be surprised by it, as if something unusual were happening to you. Instead, as you share in the sufferings of the Messiah rejoice, so that you may also rejoice with great joy at the revelation of His glory.

1 Peter 4:12-13 HCSB

We are pressured in every way but not crushed; we are perplexed but not in despair.

2 Corinthians 4:8 HCSB

Unless the Lord builds a house, its builders labor over it in vain; unless the Lord watches over a city, the watchman stays alert in vain.

Psalm 127:1 HSCB

He Watches Over Us

Have you ever faced challenges that seemed too big to handle? Have you ever faced big problems that, despite your best efforts, simply could not be solved? If so, you know how uncomfortable it is to feel helpless in the face of difficult circumstances. Thankfully, even when there's nowhere else to turn, you can turn your thoughts and prayers to God, and He will respond.

God's hand uplifts those who turn their hearts and prayers to Him. Count yourself among that number. When you do, you can live courageously and joyfully, knowing that "this too will pass"—but that God's love for you will not. And you can draw strength from the knowledge that you are a marvelous creation, loved, protected, and uplifted by the ever-present hand of God.

More Great Ideas About God's Protection

Our future may look fearfully intimidating, yet we can look up to the Engineer of the Universe, confident that nothing escapes His attention or slips out of the control of those strong hands.

Elisabeth Elliot

Through all of the crises of life—and we all are going to experience them—we have this magnificent Anchor.

Franklin Graham

My case is urgent, and I do not see how I am to be delivered; but this is no business of mine. He who makes the promise will find ways and means of keeping it. It is mine to obey His command; it is not mine to direct His counsels. I am His servant, not His solicitor. I call upon Him, and He will deliver.

C. H. Spurgeon

God delights in spreading His protective wings and enfolding His frightened, weary, beaten-down, worn-out children.

Bill Hybels

More from God's Word

The Lord bless you and protect you; the Lord make His face shine on you, and be gracious to you.

Numbers 6:24-25 HCSB

You are the God who works wonders; You revealed Your strength among the peoples.

Psalm 77:14 HCSB

Ah, Lord God! Behold, You have made the heavens and the earth by Your great power and outstretched arm. There is nothing too hard for You.

Jeremiah 32:17 NKJV

The Lord is the One who will go before you. He will be with you; He will not leave you or forsake you. Do not be afraid or discouraged.

Deuteronomy 31:8 HCSB

But the Lord will be a refuge for His people.

Joel 3:16 HCSB

Then He said to them all, "If anyone desires to come after Me, let him deny himself, and take up his cross daily, and follow Me. For whoever desires to save his life will lose it, but whoever loses his life for My sake will save it."

Luke 9:23-24 NKJV

Follow Him

J esus walks with you. Are you walking with Him? Hopefully, you will choose to walk with Him today and every day of your life.

Jesus loved you so much that He endured unspeakable humiliation and suffering for you. How will you respond to Christ's sacrifice? Will you follow the instructions of Luke 9:23 by taking up His cross and following Him? Or will you choose another path? When you place your hopes squarely at the foot of the cross, when you place Jesus squarely at the center of your life, you will be blessed. If you seek to be a worthy disciple of Jesus, you must acknowledge that He never comes "next." He is always first.

Do you hope to fulfill God's purpose for your life? Do you seek a life of abundance and peace? Do you intend to be Christian not just in name, but in deed? Then follow Christ. Follow Him by picking up His cross today and every day that you live. When you do, you will quickly discover that Christ's love has the power to change everything, including you.

"Follow Me," Jesus told them, "and I will make you into fishers of men!" Immediately they left their nets and followed Him.

—

Mark 1:17-18 HCSB

More Great Ideas About Following Jesus

The Christian faith is meant to be lived moment by moment. It isn't some broad, general outline—it's a long walk with a real Person. Details count: passing thoughts, small sacrifices, a few encouraging words, little acts of kindness, brief victories over nagging sins.

Joni Eareckson Tada

Our battles are first won or lost in the secret places of our will in God's presence, never in full view of the world.

Oswald Chambers

The essence of the Christian life is Jesus: that in all things He might have the preeminence, not that in some things He might have a place.

Franklin Graham

To walk out of His will is to walk into nowhere.

C. S. Lewis

We have in Jesus Christ a perfect example of how to put God's truth into practice.

Bill Bright

More from God's Word

The next day John saw Jesus coming toward him and said, "Here is the Lamb of God, who takes away the sin of the world!"

John 1:29 HCSB

But whoever keeps His word, truly in him the love of God is perfected. This is how we know we are in Him: the one who says he remains in Him should walk just as He walked.

1 John 2:5-6 HCSB

We encouraged, comforted, and implored each one of you to walk worthy of God, who calls you into His own kingdom and glory.

1 Thessalonians 2:12 HCSB

The one who loves his life will lose it, and the one who hates his life in this world will keep it for eternal life. If anyone serves Me, he must follow Me. Where I am, there My servant also will be. If anyone serves Me, the Father will honor him.

John 12:25-26 HCSB

If you have faith as a mustard seed, you will say to this mountain, "Move from here to there," and it will move; and nothing will be impossible for you.

Matthew 17:20 NKJV

Mountain-Moving Faith

Because we live in a demanding world, all of us have mountains to climb and mountains to move. Moving those mountains requires faith.

Are you a mountain mover whose faith is evident for all to see? Or, are you a spiritual shrinking violet? God needs more men and women who are willing to move mountains for His glory and for His kingdom.

Jesus taught His disciples that if they had faith, they could move mountains. You can too. When you place your faith, your trust, indeed your life in the hands of Christ Jesus, you'll be amazed at the marvelous things He can do. So strengthen your faith through praise, through worship, through Bible study, and through prayer. And trust God's plans. With Him, all things are possible, and He stands ready to open a world of possibilities to you . . . if you have faith.

Concentration camp survivor Corrie ten Boom relied on faith during her long months of imprisonment and torture. Later, despite the fact that four of her family members had died in Nazi death camps, Corrie's faith was unshaken. She wrote, "There is no pit so deep that God's love is not deeper still." Christians take note: Genuine faith in God means faith in all circumstances, happy or sad, joyful or tragic.

If your faith is being tested to the point of breaking, remember that your Savior is near. If you reach out to Him in faith, He will give you peace and strength. Reach out today. If you touch even the smallest fragment of the Master's garment, He will make you whole. And then, with no further ado, let the mountain moving begin.

If you do not stand firm in your faith, then you will not stand at all.

—

Isaiah 7:9 HCSB

More Great Ideas About Faith

If God chooses to remain silent, faith is content.

Ruth Bell Graham

I am truly grateful that faith enables me to move past the question of "Why?"

Zig Ziglar

When you enroll in the "school of faith," you never know what may happen next. The life of faith presents challenges that keep you going—and keep you growing!

Warren Wiersbe

Nothing is more disastrous than to study faith, analyze faith, make noble resolves of faith, but never actually to make the leap of faith.

Vance Havner

There are a lot of things in life that are difficult to understand. Faith allows the soul to go beyond what the eyes can see.

John Maxwell

So teach us to number our days, that we may gain a heart of wisdom.

Psalm 90:12 NKJV

The Gift of Life

Life is a glorious gift from God. Treat it that way. This day, like every other, is filled to the brim with opportunities, challenges, and choices. But, no choice that you make is more important than the choice you make concerning God. Today, you will either place Him at the center of your life—or not—and the consequences of that choice have implications that are both temporal and eternal.

Sometimes, we don't intentionally neglect God; we simply allow ourselves to become overwhelmed with the demands of everyday life. And then, without our even realizing it, we gradually drift away from the One we need most. Thankfully, God never drifts away from us. He remains always present, always steadfast, always loving.

As you begin this day, place God and His Son where they belong: in your head, in your prayers, on your lips, and in your heart. And then, with God as your guide and companion, let the journey begin . . .

More Great Ideas About Life

A life lived without reflection can be very superficial and empty.

Elisabeth Elliot

The whole point of this life is the healing of the heart's eye through which God is seen.

St. Augustine

Life is a gift from God, and we must treasure it, protect it, and invest it.

Warren Wiersbe

Our Lord is the Bread of Life. His proportions are perfect. There never was too much or too little of anything about Him. Feed on Him for a well-balanced ration. All the vitamins and calories are there.

Vance Havner

Jesus wants Life for us, Life with a capital L.

John Eldredge

More from God's Word

Jesus told him, "I am the way, the truth, and the life. No one comes to the Father except through Me."

John 14:6 HCSB

I urge you now to live the life to which God called you.

Ephesians 4:1 NKJV

Shout triumphantly to the Lord, all the earth. Serve the Lord with gladness; come before Him with joyful songs.

Psalm 100:1-2 HCSB

Rejoice in the Lord always. Again I will say, rejoice!

Philippians 4:4 NKJV

I have set before you life and death, blessing and curse. Choose life so that you and your descendants may live, love the Lord your God, obey Him, and remain faithful to Him. For He is your life, and He will prolong your life in the land the Lord swore to give to your fathers Abraham, Isaac, and Jacob.

Deuteronomy 30:19-20 HCSB

Go, therefore, and make disciples of all nations, baptizing them in the name of the Father and of the Son and of the Holy Spirit, teaching them to observe everything I have commanded you. And remember, I am with you always, to the end of the age.

Matthew 28:19-20 HCSB

The Great Commission

Are you a bashful Christian, one who is afraid to speak up for your Savior? Do you leave it up to others to share their testimonies while you stand on the sidelines, reluctant to share yours? Too many of us are slow to obey the last commandment of the risen Christ; we don't do our best to "make disciples of all the nations."

Christ's Great Commission applies to Christians of every generation, including our own. As believers, we are commanded to share the Good News with our families, with our neighbors, and with the world. Jesus invited His disciples to become fishers of men. We, too, must accept the Savior's invitation, and we must do so today. Tomorrow may indeed be too late.

More Great Ideas About the Great Commission

Choose Jesus Christ! Deny yourself, take up the Cross, and follow Him—for the world must be shown. The world must see, in us, a discernible, visible, startling difference.

Elisabeth Elliot

There is nothing more appealing or convincing to a watching world than to hear the testimony of someone who has just been with Jesus.

Henry Blackaby

To stand in an uncaring world and say, "See, here is the Christ" is a daring act of courage.

Calvin Miller

If we are ever going to be or do anything for our Lord, now is the time.

Vance Havner

You cannot keep silent once you have experienced salvation of Jesus Christ.

Warren Wiersbe

More from God's Word

But you will receive power when the Holy Spirit has come upon you, and you will be My witnesses in Jerusalem, in all Judea and Samaria, and to the ends of the earth.

Acts 1:8 HCSB

After this the Lord appointed 70 others, and He sent them ahead of Him in pairs to every town and place where He Himself was about to go. He told them: "The harvest is abundant, but the workers are few. Therefore, pray to the Lord of the harvest to send out workers into His harvest. Now go; I'm sending you out like lambs among wolves."

Luke 10:1-3 HCSB

Now then we are ambassadors for Christ....

2 Corinthians 5:20 KJV

You are the light of the world. A city that is set on a hill cannot be hidden. Nor do they light a lamp and put it under a basket, but on a lampstand, and it gives light to all who are in the house. Let your light so shine before men, that they may see your good works and glorify your Father in heaven.

Matthew 5:14–16 NKJV

Therefore, whether you eat or drink, or whatever you do, do all to the glory of God.

1 Corinthians 10:31 NKJV

His Priorities and Your Health

When it comes to matters of physical, spiritual, and emotional health, Christians possess an infallible guidebook: the Holy Bible. And, when it comes to matters concerning fitness—whether physical, emotional, or spiritual fitness—God's Word can help us establish clear priorities that can guide our steps and our lives.

It's easy to talk about establishing clear priorities for maintaining physical and spiritual health, but it's much more difficult to live according to those priorities. For busy believers living in a demanding world, placing first things first can be difficult indeed. Why? Because so many people are expecting so many things from us!

If you're having trouble prioritizing your day—or if you're having trouble sticking to a plan that enhances your spiritual and physical health—perhaps you've been trying to organize your life according to your own plans, not God's. A better strategy, of course, is to take your daily obligations and place them in the hands of the One who created you. To do so, you must prioritize your day according to God's commandments, and you must seek His will and His wisdom in all matters.

Would you like to embark upon a personal journey to better fitness? If so, you should remind yourself that on every step of that journey, you have a traveling companion: your Heavenly Father. Turn the concerns of this day over to Him—prayerfully, earnestly, and often. And trust Him to give you the strength you need to become the kind of person He wants you to become.

Dear friend, I pray that you may prosper in every way and be in good health, just as your soul prospers.

—

3 John 1:2 HCSB

More Great Ideas About Health

The key to healthy eating is moderation and managing what you eat every day.

John Maxwell

Ultimate healing and the glorification of the body are certainly among the blessings of Calvary for the believing Christian. Immediate healing is not guaranteed.

Warren Wiersbe

People are funny. When they are young, they will spend their health to get wealth. Later, they will gladly pay all they have trying to get their health back.

John Maxwell

If you want to form a new habit, get to work. If you want to break a bad habit, get on your knees.

Marie T. Freeman

Our primary motivation should not be for more energy or to avoid a heart attack but to please God with our bodies.

Carole Lewis

Finally, brethren, whatever things are true, whatever things are noble, whatever things are just, whatever things are pure, whatever things are lovely, whatever things are of good report, if there is any virtue and if there is anything praiseworthy— meditate on these things.

Philippians 4:8 NKJV

The Direction of Your Thoughts

How will you direct your thoughts today? Will you obey the words of Philippians 4:8 by dwelling upon those things that are true, noble, and just? Or will you allow your thoughts to be hijacked by the negativity that seems to dominate our troubled world?

Are you fearful, angry, bored, or worried? Are you so preoccupied with the concerns of this day that you fail to thank God for the promise of eternity? Are you confused, bitter, or pessimistic? If so, God wants to have a little talk with you.

God intends that you be an ambassador for Him, an enthusiastic, hope-filled Christian. But God won't force you to adopt a positive attitude. It's up to you to think positively about your blessings and opportunities . . . or not. So, today and every day hereafter, celebrate this life that God has given you by focusing your thoughts and your energies upon "things that are excellent and worthy of praise." Today, count your blessings instead of your hardships. And thank the Giver of all things good for gifts that are simply too numerous to count.

*Set your minds on what is above,
not on what is on the earth.*

—

Colossians 3:2 HCSB

More Great Ideas About Your Thoughts

The things we think are the things that feed our souls. If we think on pure and lovely things, we shall grow pure and lovely like them; and the converse is equally true.

Hannah Whitall Smith

Your thoughts are the determining factor as to whose mold you are conformed to. Control your thoughts and you control the direction of your life.

Charles Stanley

Beware of cut-and-dried theologies that reduce the ways of God to a manageable formula that keeps life safe. God often does the unexplainable just to keep us on our toes—and also on our knees.

Warren Wiersbe

Every major spiritual battle is in the mind.

Charles Stanley

It is the thoughts and intents of the heart that shape a person's life.

John Eldredge

Whoever conceals an offense promotes love, but whoever gossips about it separates friends.

Proverbs 17:9 HCSB

Above and Beyond Gossip

The Bible clearly tells us that gossip is wrong. But when it comes to the special confidences that you share with your very closest friends, gossip can be disastrous.

The Bible reminds us that "Reckless words pierce like a sword, but the tongue of the wise brings healing" (Proverbs 12:18 NIV). Therefore, if we are to solve more problems than we start, we must measure our words carefully, and we must never betray a confidence. But sometimes even the most thoughtful among us may speak first and think second (with decidedly mixed results).

When we speak too quickly, we may say things that that would be better left unsaid. When we forgo the wonderful opportunity to consider our thoughts before we give voice to them, we're putting ourselves and our relationships in danger.

A far better strategy, of course, is to do the more difficult thing: to think first and to speak next. When we do so, we give ourselves ample time to compose our thoughts and to consult our Creator before we say something that we might soon regret.

More Great Ideas About Gossip

I still believe we ought to talk about Jesus. The old country doctor of my boyhood days always began his examination by saying, "Let me see your tongue." That's a good way to check a Christian: the tongue test. Let's hear what he is talking about.

Vance Havner

Change the heart, and you change the speech.

Warren Wiersbe

The great test of a man's character is his tongue.

Oswald Chambers

Fill the heart with the love of Christ so that only truth and purity can come out of the mouth.

Warren Wiersbe

Rejoice in the Lord always. Again I will say, rejoice!

Philippians 4:4 NKJV

Rejoice!

Are you living a life of agitation, consternation, or celebration? If you're a believer, it should most certainly be the latter. With Christ as your Savior, every day should be a time of celebration.

Oswald Chambers correctly observed, "Joy is the great note all throughout the Bible." C. S. Lewis echoed that thought when he wrote, "Joy is the serious business of heaven." But, even the most dedicated Christians can, on occasion, forget to celebrate each day for what it is: a priceless gift from God.

Today, celebrate the life that God has given you. Today, put a smile on your face, kind words on your lips, and a song in your heart. Be generous with your praise and free with your encouragement. And then, when you have celebrated life to the fullest, invite your friends to do likewise. After all, this is God's day, and He has given us clear instructions for its use. We are commanded to rejoice and be glad.

More Great Ideas About Celebration

Joy is a by-product not of happy circumstances, education or talent, but of a healthy relationship with God and a determination to love Him no matter what.

Barbara Johnson

A life of intimacy with God is characterized by joy.

Oswald Chambers

When we get rid of inner conflicts and wrong attitudes toward life, we will almost automatically burst into joy.

E. Stanley Jones

Some of us seem so anxious about avoiding hell that we forget to celebrate our journey toward heaven.

Philip Yancey

Joy is the direct result of having God's perspective on our daily lives and the effect of loving our Lord enough to obey His commands and trust His promises.

Bill Bright

More from God's Word

This is the day the LORD has made; we will rejoice and be glad in it.

Psalm 118:24 NKJV

If they serve Him obediently, they will end their days in prosperity and their years in happiness.

Job 36:11 HCSB

The one who understands a matter finds success, and the one who trusts in the Lord will be happy.

Proverbs 16:20 HCSB

A joyful heart is good medicine, but a broken spirit dries up the bones.

Proverbs 17:22 HCSB

How happy is the man who does not follow the advice of the wicked, or take the path of sinners, or join a group of mockers!

Psalm 1:1 HCSB

I have set before you life and death, blessing and curse. Choose life so that you and your descendants may live, love the Lord your God, obey Him, and remain faithful to Him. For He is your life, and He will prolong your life in the land the Lord swore to give to your fathers Abraham, Isaac, and Jacob.

Deuteronomy 30:19-20 HCSB

Making Good Choices

Life is a series of choices. From the instant we wake in the morning until the moment we nod off to sleep at night, we make countless decisions: decisions about the things we do, decisions about the words we speak, and decisions about the thoughts we choose to think. Simply put, the quality of those decisions determines the quality of our lives.

As believers who have been saved by a loving and merciful God, we have every reason to make wise choices. Yet sometimes, amid the inevitable hustle and bustle of life here on earth, we allow ourselves to behave in ways that we know are displeasing to God. When we do, we forfeit—albeit temporarily—the joy and the peace that we might otherwise experience through Him.

As you consider the next step in your life's journey, take time to consider how many things in this life you

100 Verses for Your Journey

can control: your thoughts, your words, your priorities, and your actions, for starters. And then, if you sincerely want to discover God's purpose for your life, make choices that are pleasing to Him. He deserves no less . . . and neither do you.

*So I strive always to keep
my conscience clear
before God and man.*

—

Acts 24:16 NIV

171

More Great Ideas About Choices

Every day, I find countless opportunities to decide whether I will obey God and demonstrate my love for Him or try to please myself or the world system. God is waiting for my choices.

Bill Bright

Every time you make a choice, you are turning the central part of you, the part that chooses, into something a little different from what it was before.

C. S. Lewis

Life is pretty much like a cafeteria line—it offers us many choices, both good and bad. The Christian must have a spiritual radar that detects the difference not only between bad and good but also among good, better, and best.

Dennis Swanberg

We are either the masters or the victims of our attitudes. It is a matter of personal choice. Who we are today is the result of choices we made yesterday. Tomorrow, we will become what we choose today. To change means to choose to change.

John Maxwell

As the Father loved Me, I also have loved you; abide in My love.

John 15:9 NKJV

Christ's Love

How much does Christ love us? More than we, as mere mortals, can comprehend. His love is perfect and steadfast. Even though we are fallible and wayward, the Good Shepherd cares for us still. Even though we have fallen far short of the Father's commandments, Christ loves us with a power and depth that are beyond our understanding. The sacrifice that Jesus made upon the cross was made for each of us, and His love endures to the edge of eternity and beyond.

Hannah Whitall Smith spoke to believers of every generation when she advised, "Keep your face upturned to Christ as the flowers do to the sun. Look, and your soul shall live and grow." How true. When we turn our hearts to Jesus, we receive His blessings, His peace, and His grace.

Christ is the ultimate Savior of mankind and the personal Savior of those who believe in Him. As His servants, we should place Him at the very center of our lives. And, every day that God gives us breath, we should share Christ's love and His message with a world that needs both.

Christ's love changes everything. When you accept His gift of grace, you are transformed, not only for today, but also for all eternity. If you haven't already done so, accept Jesus Christ as your personal Savior. He's waiting patiently for you to invite Him into your heart. Please don't make Him wait a single minute longer.

No one has greater love than this, that someone would lay down his life for his friends.

—

John 15:13 HCSB

More Great Ideas About Christ's Love

Sometimes Agape really hurts. It broke the heart of God to demonstrate His love to us through Christ but its ultimate end was salvation.

Beth Moore

Christ is like a river that is continually flowing. There are always fresh supplies of water coming from the fountainhead, so that a man may live by it and be supplied with water all his life. So Christ is an ever-flowing fountain; he is continually supplying his people, and the fountain is not spent. They who live upon Christ may have fresh supplies from him for all eternity; they may have an increase of blessedness that is new, and new still, and which never will come to an end.

Jonathan Edwards

Jesus: the proof of God's love.

Philip Yancey

No man ever loved like Jesus. He taught the blind to see and the dumb to speak. He died on the cross to save us. He bore our sins. And now God says, "Because He did, I can forgive you."

Billy Graham

Rejoice always, pray without ceasing, in everything give thanks; for this is the will of God in Christ Jesus for you.

1 Thessalonians 5:16-18 NKJV

Pray Often

Is prayer an integral part of your daily life, or is it a hit-or-miss habit? Do you "pray without ceasing," or is your prayer life an afterthought? Do you regularly pray in the quiet moments of the early morning, or do you bow your head only when others are watching?

As Christians, we are instructed to pray often. But it is important to note that genuine prayer requires much more than bending our knees and closing our eyes. Heartfelt prayer is an attitude of the heart.

If your prayers have become more a matter of habit than a matter of passion, you're robbing yourself of a deeper relationship with God. And how can you rectify this situation? By praying more frequently and more fervently. When you do, God will shower you with His blessings, His grace, and His love.

The quality of your spiritual life will be in direct proportion to the quality of your prayer life: the more you pray, the closer you will feel to God. So today, instead of turning things over in your mind, turn them over to God in prayer. Instead of worrying about your next decision, ask God to lead the way. Don't limit your prayers to the dinner table or the bedside table. Pray constantly about things great and small. God is always listening; it's up to you to do the rest.

More Great Ideas About Prayer

Obedience is the master key to effective prayer.

Billy Graham

Prayer may not get us what we want, but it will teach us to want what we need.

Vance Havner

Learn to pray to God in such a way that you are trusting Him as your Physician to do what He knows is best. Confess to Him the disease, and let Him choose the remedy.

St. Augustine

Those who know God the best are the richest and most powerful in prayer. Little acquaintance with God, and strangeness and coldness to Him, make prayer a rare and feeble thing.

E. M. Bounds

Be an example to the believers in word, in conduct, in love, in spirit, in faith, in purity.

1 Timothy 4:12 NKJV

Being the Right Kind of Example

Whether we like it or not, all of us are role models. Our friends and family members watch our actions and, as followers of Christ, we are obliged to act accordingly.

What kind of example are you? Are you the kind of person whose life serves as a genuine example of righteousness? Are you a person whose behavior serves as a positive role model for others? Are you the kind of person whose actions, day in and day out, are based upon kindness, faithfulness, and a love for the Lord? If so, you are not only blessed by God, but you are also a powerful force for good in a world that desperately needs positive influences such as yours.

We live in a dangerous, temptation-filled world. That's why you encounter so many opportunities to stray from God's commandments. Resist those temptations! When you do, you'll earn God's blessings and you'll serve as a positive role model for your family and friends.

Corrie ten Boom advised, "Don't worry about what you do not understand. Worry about what you do understand in the Bible but do not live by." And that's sound advice because our families and friends are watching . . . and so, for that matter, is God.

*Set an example of good works yourself,
with integrity and dignity
in your teaching.*

—

Titus 2:7 HCSB

More Great Ideas About
Setting the Right Kind of Example

If I take care of my character, my reputation will take care of itself.

D. L. Moody

There is no way to grow a saint overnight. Character, like the oak tree, does not spring up like a mushroom.

Vance Havner

You can never separate a leader's actions from his character.

John Maxwell

More depends on my walk than my talk.

D. L. Moody

Among the most joyful people I have known have been some who seem to have had no human reason for joy. The sweet fragrance of Christ has shown through their lives.

Elisabeth Elliot

Now godliness with contentment is great gain. For we brought nothing into this world, and it is certain we can carry nothing out. And having food and clothing, with these we shall be content.

1 Timothy 6:6-8 NKJV

Keep It Simple

You live in a world where simplicity is in short supply. Think for a moment about the complexity of your everyday life and compare it to the lives of your ancestors. Certainly, you are the beneficiary of many technological innovations, but those innovations have a price: in all likelihood, your world is highly complex. Consider the following:

1. From the moment you wake up in the morning until the time you lay your head on the pillow at night, you are the target of an endless stream of advertising information. Each message is intended to grab your attention in order to convince you to purchase things you didn't know you needed (and probably don't!).

2. Essential aspects of your life, including personal matters such as health care, are subject to an ever-increasing flood of rules and regulations.

3. Unless you take firm control of your time and your life, you may be overwhelmed by an ever-increasing tidal wave of complexity that threatens your happiness.

Your Heavenly Father understands the joy of living simply, and so should you. So do yourself a favor: keep your life as simple as possible. Simplicity is, indeed, genius. By simplifying your life, you are destined to improve it.

More Great Ideas About Simplicity

All that a Christian does, even in eating and sleeping, is prayer, when it is done in simplicity, according to the order of God, without either adding to or diminishing from it by His choice.

John Wesley

The fewer words, the better prayer.

Martin Luther

The most powerful life is the most simple life. The most powerful life is the life that knows where it's going, that knows where the source of strength is; it is the life that stays free of clutter and happenstance and hurriedness.

Max Lucado

Draw near to God, and He will draw near to you.

James 4:8 HCSB

Draw Near to God

If God is everywhere, why does He sometimes seem so far away? The answer to that question, of course, has nothing to do with God and everything to do with us.

When we begin each day on our knees, in praise and worship to Him, God often seems very near indeed. But, if we ignore God's presence or—worse yet—rebel against it altogether, the world in which we live becomes a spiritual wasteland.

Are you tired, discouraged, or fearful? Be comforted because God is with you. Are you confused? Listen to the quiet voice of your Heavenly Father. Are you bitter? Talk with God and seek His guidance. Are you celebrating a great victory? Thank God and praise Him. He is the Giver of all things good.

In whatever condition you find yourself, wherever you are, whether you are happy or sad, victorious or vanquished, troubled or triumphant, celebrate God's presence. And be comforted. God is not just near; He has promised that He is right here, right now. And that's a promise you can depend on.

More Great Ideas About God's Presence

The next time you hear a baby laugh or see an ocean wave, take note. Pause and listen as his Majesty whispers ever so gently, "I'm here."

Max Lucado

Get into the habit of dealing with God about everything. Unless, in the first waking moment of the day you learn to fling the door wide back and let God in, you will work on a wrong level all day. But, swing the door wide open and pray to your Father in secret, and every public thing will be stamped with the presence of God.

Oswald Chambers

There is a basic urge: the longing for unity. You desire a reunion with God—with God your Father.

E. Stanley Jones

God does not dispense strength and encouragement like a druggist fills your prescription. The Lord doesn't promise to give us something to take so we can handle our weary moments. He promises us Himself. That is all. And that is enough.

Charles Swindoll

The borrower is servant to the lender.

Proverbs 22:7 NIV

Beware of Debt

We live in a world that is addicted to debt, but you needn't be. Just because our world revolves around borrowed money doesn't mean that you must do likewise.

If you're already living beyond your means and borrowing to pay for the privilege, then you know that sleepless nights and stress-filled days are the psychological payments that must be extracted from those who buy too much "now" in hopes that they can pay for those things "later." Unfortunately, "later" usually arrives sooner than expected, and that's when the trouble begins.

Whether you're buying a mattress, a microwave, or a Maserati, somebody will probably be willing to sell it to you on credit. But the Bible makes it clear that the instant you become a debtor, you also become a servant to the lender. So if you're trying to decide whether or not to make that next big purchase, remember that when it comes to borrowed money, less is usually more . . . much more.

More Great Ideas About Debt

Having money may not make people happy, but owing money is sure to make them miserable.

John Maxwell

God says that when you borrow, you become a servant of the lender; the lender is established as an authority over the borrower. (Proverbs 22:7)

Larry Burkett

There is absolutely no evidence that complexity and materialism lead to happiness. On the contrary, there is plenty of evidence that simplicity and spirituality lead to joy, a blessedness that is better than happiness.

Dennis Swanberg

Nobody is going to simplify your life for you. You've got to simplify things for yourself.

Marie T. Freeman

Getting out of the pit requires we surround ourselves with people who love us enough to support us and lift us up when we are at our ugliest.

Dave Ramsey

He did it with all his heart. So he prospered.

2 Chronicles 31:21 NKJV

Putting Yourself and Your Heart into Your Work

The old adage is both familiar and true: We must pray as if everything depended upon God, but work as if everything depended upon us. Yet sometimes, when we are weary and discouraged, we may allow our worries to sap our energy and our hope. God has other intentions. God intends that we pray for things, and He intends that we be willing to work for the things that we pray for. More importantly, God intends that our work should become His work.

Whether you're in school or in the workplace, your success will depend, in large part, upon the passion that you bring to your work. God has created a world in which diligence is rewarded and sloth is not. So whatever you choose to do, do it with commitment, with excitement, with enthusiasm, and with vigor.

God did not create you for a life of mediocrity; He created you for far greater things. Reaching for greater things usually requires work and lots of it, which is perfectly fine with God. After all, He knows that you're up to the task, and He has big plans for you. Very big plans…

More Great Ideas About Passion

We honor God by asking for great things when they are part of His promise. We dishonor Him and cheat ourselves when we ask for molehills where He has offered mountains.

Vance Havner

One of the great needs in the church today is for every Christian to become enthusiastic about his faith in Jesus Christ.

Billy Graham

When we wholeheartedly commit ourselves to God, there is nothing mediocre or run-of-the-mill about us. To live for Christ is to be passionate about our Lord and about our lives.

Jim Gallery

Everything you love is what makes a life worth living.

John Eldredge

So rid yourselves of all wickedness, all deceit, hypocrisy, envy, and all slander.

1 Peter 2:1 HCSB

Beyond Envy

Because we are frail, imperfect human beings, we are sometimes envious of others. But God's Word warns us that envy is sin. Thus, we must guard ourselves against the natural tendency to feel resentment and jealousy when other people experience good fortune.

As believers, we have absolutely no reason to be envious of any people on earth. After all, as Christians we are already recipients of the greatest gift in all creation: God's grace. We have been promised the gift of eternal life through God's only begotten Son, and we must count that gift as our most precious possession.

Rather than succumbing to the sin of envy, we should focus on the marvelous things that God has done for us—starting with Christ's sacrifice. And we must refrain from preoccupying ourselves with the blessings that God has chosen to give others.

So here's a surefire formula for a happier, healthier life: Count your own blessings and let your neighbors count theirs. It's the godly way to live.

More Great Ideas About Envy

When you worry about what you don't have, you won't be able to enjoy what you do have.

Charles Swindoll

What God asks, does, or requires of others is not my business; it is His.

Kay Arthur

Discontent dries up the soul.

Elisabeth Elliot

Contentment comes when we develop an attitude of gratitude for the important things we do have in our lives that we tend to take for granted if we have our eyes staring longingly at our neighbor's stuff.

Dave Ramsey

How can you possess the miseries of envy when you possess in Christ the best of all portions?

C. H. Spurgeon

More from God's Word

Do not covet your neighbor's house . . . or anything that belongs to your neighbor.

Exodus 20:17 HCSB

We must not become conceited, provoking one another, envying one another.

Galatians 5:26 HCSB

For where envy and selfish ambition exist, there is disorder and every kind of evil.

James 3:16 HCSB

Then I observed that most people are motivated to success by their envy of their neighbors. But this, too, is meaningless, like chasing the wind.

Ecclesiastes 4:4 NLT

A tranquil heart is life to the body, but jealousy is rottenness to the bones.

Proverbs 14:30 HCSB

Therefore, submit to God. But resist the Devil, and he will flee from you. Draw near to God, and He will draw near to you. Cleanse your hands, sinners, and purify your hearts, double-minded people!

James 4:7-8 HCSB

Beware of the Adversary

This world is God's creation, and it contains the wonderful fruits of His handiwork. But, the world also contains countless opportunities to stray from God's will. Temptations are everywhere, and the devil, it seems, never takes a day off. Our task, as believers, is to turn away from temptation and to place our lives squarely in the center of God's will.

In his letter to Jewish Christians, Peter offered a stern warning: "Your adversary, the devil, prowls around like a roaring lion, seeking someone to devour" (1 Peter 5:8 NASB). What was true in New Testament times is equally true in our own. Evil is indeed abroad in the world, and Satan continues to sow the seeds of destruction far and wide. As Christians, we must guard our hearts by earnestly wrapping ourselves in the protection of God's Holy Word. When we do, we are protected.

More Great Ideas About Evil

There is nothing evil in matter itself. Evil lies in the spirit. Evils of the heart, of the mind, of the soul, of the spirit—these have to do with man's sin, and the only reason the human body does evil is because the human spirit uses it to do evil.

A. W. Tozer

Christianity isn't a religion about going to Sunday school, potluck suppers, being nice, holding car washes, sending your secondhand clothes off to Mexico—as good as those things might be. This is a world at war.

John Eldredge

The descent to hell is easy, and those who begin by worshipping power soon worship evil.

C. S. Lewis

Of two evils, choose neither.

C. H. Spurgeon

God loves you, and He yearns for you to turn away from the path of evil. You need His forgiveness, and you need Him to come into your life and remake you from within.

Billy Graham

More from God's Word

Do not be conquered by evil, but conquer evil with good.

Romans 12:21 HCSB

For everyone who practices wicked things hates the light and avoids it, so that his deeds may not be exposed. But anyone who lives by the truth comes to the light, so that his works may be shown to be accomplished by God.

John 3:20–21 HCSB

He replied, "Every plant that My heavenly Father didn't plant will be uprooted."

Matthew 15:13 HCSB

But the path of the just is like the shining sun, that shines ever brighter unto the perfect day. The way of the wicked is like darkness; they do not know what makes them stumble.

Proverbs 4:18-19 NKJV

Don't consider yourself to be wise; fear the Lord and turn away from evil.

Proverbs 3:7 HCSB

Give thanks to the Lord, for He is good; His faithful love endures forever.

Psalm 106:1 HCSB

His Love Endures

God's love for you is bigger and better than you can imagine. In fact, God's love is far too big to comprehend (in this lifetime). But this much we know: God loves you so much that He sent His Son Jesus to come to this earth and to die for you. And, when you accepted Jesus into your heart, God gave you a gift that is more precious than gold: the gift of eternal life. Now, precisely because you are a wondrous creation treasured by God, a question presents itself: What will you do in response to God's love? Will you ignore it or embrace it? Will you return it or neglect it? The decision, of course, is yours and yours alone.

When you embrace God's love, you are forever changed. When you embrace God's love, you feel differently about yourself, your neighbors, and your world. When you embrace God's love, you share His message and you obey His commandments.

When you accept the Father's gift of grace, you are blessed here on earth and throughout all eternity. So do yourself a favor right now: accept God's love with open arms and welcome His Son Jesus into your heart. When you do, your life will be changed today, tomorrow, and forever.

For the Lord is good,
and His love is eternal;
His faithfulness endures through
all generations.

—

Psalm 100:5 HCSB

More Great Ideas About God's Love

The hope we have in Jesus is the anchor for the soul—something sure and steadfast, preventing drifting or giving way, lowered to the depth of God's love.

Franklin Graham

Every tiny bit of my life that has value I owe to the redemption of Jesus Christ. Am I doing anything to enable Him to bring His redemption into evident reality in the lives of others?

Oswald Chambers

Even when we cannot see the why and wherefore of God's dealings, we know that there is love in and behind them, so we can rejoice always.

J. I. Packer

God proved his love on the cross. When Christ hung, and bled, and died, it was God saying to the world—I love you.

Billy Graham

No temptation has overtaken you except such as is common to man; but God is faithful, who will not allow you to be tempted beyond what you are able, but with the temptation will also make the way of escape, that you may be able to bear it.

1 Corinthians 10:13 NKJV

Resisting Temptation

It's inevitable: today you will be tempted by somebody or something—in fact, you will probably be tempted many times. Why? Because you live in a world that is filled to the brim with temptations! Some of these temptations are small; eating a second scoop of ice cream, for example, is enticing but not very dangerous. Other temptations, however, are not nearly so harmless.

The devil is working 24/7, and he's causing pain and heartache in more ways than ever before. We, as believers, must remain watchful and strong. And the good news is this: When it comes to fighting Satan, we are never alone. God is always with us, and He gives us the power to resist temptation whenever we ask Him to give us strength.

More Great Ideas About Temptation

In the worst temptations nothing can help us but faith that God's Son has put on flesh, sits at the right hand of the Father, and prays for us. There is no mightier comfort.

Martin Luther

Most Christians do not know or fully realize that the adversary of our lives is Satan and that his main tool is our flesh, our old nature.

Bill Bright

There is sharp necessity for giving Christ absolute obedience. The devil bids for our complete self-will. To whatever extent we give this self-will the right to be master over our lives, we are, to an extent, giving Satan a toehold.

Catherine Marshall

A man who gives in to temptation after five minutes simply does not know what it would have been like an hour later.

C. S. Lewis

Blessed are those who hunger and thirst for righteousness, because they will be filled.

Matthew 5:6 HCSB

Living Righteously

Matthew 5:6 teaches us that righteous men and women are blessed. Do you sincerely desire to be a righteous person? Are you bound and determined—despite the inevitable temptations and distractions of our modern age—to be an example of godly behavior to your family, to your friends, to your coworkers, and to your community? If so, you must obey God's commandments. There are no shortcuts and no loopholes—to be a faithful Christian, you must be an obedient Christian.

You will never become righteous by accident. You must hunger for righteousness, and you must ask God to guide your steps. When you ask Him for guidance, He will give it. So, when you're faced with a difficult choice or a powerful temptation, seek God's counsel and trust the counsel He gives. Invite God into your heart and live according to His commandments. When you do, you will be blessed today, tomorrow, and forever.

More Great Ideas About Doing What's Right

Righteousness not only defines God, but God defines righteousness.

Bill Hybels

Have your heart right with Christ, and he will visit you often, and so turn weekdays into Sundays, meals into sacraments, homes into temples, and earth into heaven.

C. H. Spurgeon

A man who lives right, and is right, has more power in his silence than another has by his words.

Phillips Brooks

The great thing is to be found at one's post as a child of God, living each day as though it were our last, but planning as though our world might last a hundred years.

C. S. Lewis

Our afflictions are designed not to break us but to bend us toward the eternal and the holy.

Barbara Johnson

Therefore humble yourselves under the mighty hand of God, that He may exalt you in due time, casting all your care upon Him, for He cares for you.

1 Peter 5:6-7 NKJV

He Cares

It is easy to become overwhelmed by the demands of everyday life, but if you're a faithful follower of the One from Galilee, you need never be overwhelmed. Why? Because God's love is sufficient to meet your needs. Whatever dangers you may face, whatever heartbreaks you must endure, God is with you, and He stands ready to comfort you and to heal you.

The Psalmist writes, "Weeping may endure for a night, but joy comes in the morning" (Psalm 30:5 NKJV). But when we are suffering, the morning may seem very far away. It is not. God promises that He is "near to those who have a broken heart" (Psalm 34:18 NKJV).

If you are experiencing the intense pain of a recent loss, or if you are still mourning a loss from long ago, perhaps you are now ready to begin the next stage of your journey with God. If so, be mindful of this fact: the loving heart of God is sufficient to meet any challenge, including yours.

More Great Ideas About God's Support

How delightful a teacher, but gentle a provider, how bountiful a giver is my Father! Praise, praise to Thee, O manifested Most High.

Jim Elliot

We should learn to live in the presence of the living God. He should be a well for us: delightful, comforting, unfailing, springing up to eternal life (John 4:14). When we rely on other people, their water supplies ultimately dry up. But, the well of the Creator never fails to nourish us.

C. H. Spurgeon

God is bigger than your problems. Whatever worries press upon you today, put them in God's hands and leave them there.

Billy Graham

God uses our most stumbling, faltering faith-steps as the open door to His doing for us "more than we ask or think."

Catherine Marshall

In the same way faith, if it doesn't have works, is dead by itself.

James 2:17 HCSB

Faith Without Works Doesn't Work

The central message of James' letter is the need for believers to act upon their beliefs. James' instruction is clear: "faith without works is dead." We are saved by our faith in Christ, but salvation does not signal the end of our earthly responsibilities; it marks the true beginning of our work for the Lord.

If your faith in God is strong, you will find yourself drawn toward God's work. You will serve Him, not just with words or prayers, but also with deeds. Because of your faith, you will feel compelled to do God's work—to do it gladly, faithfully, joyfully, and consistently.

Today, redouble your efforts to do God's bidding here on earth. Never have the needs—or the opportunities—been greater.

More Great Ideas About Good Works

The religion of Jesus Christ has an ethical as well as a doctrinal side.

Lottie Moon

We are saved by faith alone, but faith is never alone.

John Calvin

Where there are no good works, there is no faith. If works and love do not blossom forth, it is not genuine faith, the Gospel has not yet gained a foothold, and Christ is not yet rightly known.

Martin Luther

It is faith that saves us, not works, but the faith that saves us always produces works.

C. H. Spurgeon

Those who make religion consist altogether in good works overlook the fact that works themselves are not acceptable to God unless they proceed from faith. For without faith, it is impossible to please Him. And those who make religion consist altogether in faith overlook the fact that true faith always works by love, and invariably produces the works of love.

Charles Finney

In all your ways acknowledge Him, and He shall direct your paths.

Proverbs 3:6 NKJV

Seeking God's Guidance

When we genuinely seek to know the heart of God—when we prayerfully seek His wisdom and His will—our Heavenly Father carefully guides us over the peaks and valleys of life. And as Christians, we can be comforted: Whether we find ourselves at the pinnacle of the mountain or the darkest depths of the valley, the loving heart of God is always there with us.

As Christians whose salvation has been purchased by the blood of Christ, we have every reason to live joyously and courageously. After all, Christ has already fought and won our battle for us—He did so on the cross at Calvary. But despite Christ's sacrifice, and despite God's promises, we may become confused or disoriented by the endless complications and countless distractions of everyday life.

If you're unsure of your next step, lean upon God's promises and lift your prayers to Him. Remember that God is always near; remember that He is your protector and your deliverer. Open yourself to His heart, and trust Him to guide your path. When you do, God will direct your steps, and you will receive His blessings today, tomorrow, and throughout eternity.

Teach me Your way, Lord,
and I will live by Your truth.
Give me an undivided mind
to fear Your name.

—

Psalm 86:11 HCSB

More Great Ideas About God's Guidance

Are you serious about wanting God's guidance to become a personal reality in your life? The first step is to tell God that you know you can't manage your own life; that you need his help.

Catherine Marshall

If we want to hear God's voice, we must surrender our minds and hearts to Him.

Billy Graham

Walk in the daylight of God's will because then you will be safe; you will not stumble.

Anne Graham Lotz

It is a joy that God never abandons His children. He guides faithfully all who listen to His directions.

Corrie ten Boom

Enjoy the adventure of receiving God guidance. Taste it, revel in it, appreciate the fact that the journey is often a lot more exciting than arriving at the destination.

Bill Hybels

But this I say: He who sows sparingly will also reap sparingly, and he who sows bountifully will also reap bountifully. So let each one give as he purposes in his heart, not grudgingly or of necessity; for God loves a cheerful giver.

2 Corinthians 9:6-7 NKJV

Generosity Now

The thread of generosity is woven—completely and inextricably—into the very fabric of Christ's teachings. As He sent His disciples out to heal the sick and spread God's message of salvation, Jesus offered this guiding principle: "Freely you have received, freely give" (Matthew 10:8 NIV). The principle still applies. If we are to be disciples of Christ, we must give freely of our time, our possessions, and our love.

In 2 Corinthians 9, Paul reminds us that when we sow the seeds of generosity, we reap bountiful rewards in accordance with God's plan for our lives. Thus, we are instructed to give cheerfully and without reservation. So today, make this pledge and keep it: Be a cheerful, generous, courageous giver. The world needs your help, and you need the spiritual rewards that will be yours when you give it.

More Great Ideas About Generosity

God does not need our money. But, you and I need the experience of giving it.

James Dobson

The happiest and most joyful people are those who give money and serve.

Dave Ramsey

Abundant living means abundant giving.

E. Stanley Jones

God does not supply money to satisfy our every whim and desire. His promise is to meet our needs and provide an abundance so that we can help other people.

Larry Burkett

The measure of a life, after all, is not its duration but its donation.

Corrie ten Boom

Should we accept only good from God and not adversity?

Job 2:10 HCSB

Learning the Art of Acceptance

I f you're like most people, you like being in control. Period. You want things to happen according to your wishes and according to your timetable. But sometimes, God has other plans . . . and He always has the final word. Job understood the importance of accepting God's sovereignty in good times and bad . . . and so should you.

The American theologian Reinhold Niebuhr composed a profoundly simple verse that came to be known as the Serenity Prayer: "God, grant me the serenity to accept the things I cannot change, the courage to change the things I can, and the wisdom to know the difference." Niebuhr's words are far easier to recite than they are to live by.

Oswald Chambers correctly observed, "Our Lord never asks us to decide for Him; He asks us to yield to Him—a very different matter." These words remind us that even when we cannot understand the workings of God, we must trust Him and accept His will.

Are you embittered by a personal tragedy that you did not deserve and cannot understand? If so, it's time to make peace with life. It's time to forgive others, and, if necessary, to forgive yourself. It's time to accept the unchangeable past, to embrace the priceless present, and to have faith in the promise of tomorrow. It's time to trust God completely. And it's time to reclaim the peace—His peace—that can and should be yours.

So if you've encountered unfortunate circumstances that are beyond your power to control, accept those circumstances . . . and trust God. When you do, you can be comforted in the knowledge that your Creator is both loving and wise, and that He understands His plans perfectly, even when you do not.

For everything created by God is good, and nothing should be rejected if it is received with thanksgiving.

—

1 Timothy 4:4 HCSB

More Great Ideas About Acceptance

Tomorrow's job is fathered by today's acceptance. Acceptance of what, at least for the moment, you cannot alter.

Max Lucado

Faith in God will not get for you everything you want, but it will get for you what God wants you to have. The unbeliever does not need what he wants; the Christian should want only what he needs.

Vance Havner

Our Lord never asks us to decide for Him; He asks us to yield to Him—a very different matter.

Oswald Chambers

Trust the past to God's mercy, the present to God's love, and the future to God's providence.

St. Augustine

When we face an impossible situation, all self-reliance and self-confidence must melt away; we must be totally dependent on Him for the resources.

Anne Graham Lotz

Acquire wisdom—how much better it is than gold! And acquire understanding—it is preferable to silver.

Proverbs 16:16 HCSB

Acquiring Wisdom

Proverbs 16:16 teaches us that wisdom is more valuable than gold. All of us would like to be wise, but not all of us are willing to do the work that is required to become wise. Wisdom is not like a mushroom; it does not spring up overnight. It is, instead, like an oak tree that starts as a tiny acorn, grows into a sapling, and eventually reaches up to the sky, tall and strong.

To become wise, we must seek God's wisdom and live according to His Word. To become wise, we must seek wisdom with consistency and purpose. To become wise, we must not only learn the lessons of the Christian life, we must also live by them.

Do you seek to live a life of righteousness and wisdom? If so, you must study the ultimate source of wisdom: the Word of God. You must seek out worthy mentors and listen carefully to their advice. You must associate, day in and day out, with godly men and women. Then, as you accumulate wisdom, you must not keep it for yourself; you must, instead, share it with your friends and family members.

But be forewarned: if you sincerely seek to share your hard-earned wisdom with others, your actions must give credence to your words. The best way to share one's wisdom—perhaps the only way—is not by words, but by example.

More Great Ideas About Wisdom

Knowledge is horizontal. Wisdom is vertical; it comes down from above.

Billy Graham

God's plan for our guidance is for us to grow gradually in wisdom before we get to the cross roads.

Bill Hybels

The more wisdom enters our hearts, the more we will be able to trust our hearts in difficult situations.

John Eldredge

If we neglect the Bible, we cannot expect to benefit from the wisdom and direction that result from knowing God's Word.

Vonette Bright

But the fruit of the Spirit is love, joy, peace, patience, kindness, goodness, faith, gentleness, self-control. Against such things there is no law.

Galatians 5:22-23 HCSB

The Fruit of the Spirit

In Galatians 5, we are also told that when people live by the Spirit, they will bear "fruit of the Spirit." But what, exactly, is the fruit of the Spirit? It's a way of behaving yourself, a way of treating other people, a way of showing the world what it means to be a Christian. The Bible says, "The fruit of the Spirit is love, joy, peace, patience, kindness, goodness, faith, gentleness, self-control."

Today and every day, will you strive to be patient, joyful, loving, and kind? Will you really try to control yourself? And while you're at it, will you be peaceful, gentle, patient, and faithful? If so, you'll demonstrate to the world that the fruit of the Spirit can make a wonderful difference in the lives of good Christian people—people like you!

More Great Ideas About the Fruit of the Spirit

Some people have received Christ but have never reached spiritual maturity. We should grow as Christians every day, and we are not completely mature until we live in the presence of Christ.

Billy Graham

Though we, as Christians, are like Christ, having the first fruits of the Spirit, we are unlike Him, having the remainders of the flesh.

Thomas Watson

The Holy Spirit cannot be located as a guest in a house. He invades everything.

Oswald Chambers

The Holy Spirit is like a living and continually flowing fountain in believers. We have the boundless privilege of tapping into that fountain every time we pray.

Shirley Dobson

The more we abide in Christ, the more fruit we bear.

Warren Wiersbe

More from God's Word

There are diversities of gifts, but the same Spirit.

1 Corinthians 12:4 NKJV

And don't get drunk with wine, which leads to reckless actions, but be filled with the Spirit.

Ephesians 5:18 HCSB

So this is the point: The law no longer holds you in its power, because you died to its power when you died with Christ on the cross. And now you are united with the one who was raised from the dead. As a result, you can produce good fruit, that is, good deeds for God.

Romans 7:4 NLT

And when they had prayed, the place was shaken where they were assembled together; and they were all filled with the Holy Ghost, and they spake the word of God with boldness.

Acts 4:31 KJV

A good person produces good deeds and words season after season.

Matthew 12:35 MSG

We are hard pressed on every side, yet not crushed; we are perplexed, but not in despair.

2 Corinthians 4:8 NKJV

Beyond Discouragement

We Christians have many reasons to celebrate. God is in His heaven; Christ has risen, and we are the sheep of His flock. Yet sometimes, even the most devout believers may become discouraged. After all, we live in a world where expectations can be high and demands can be even higher.

When we fail to meet the expectations of others (or, for that matter, the expectations that we have for ourselves), we may be tempted to abandon hope. But God has other plans. He knows exactly how He intends to use us. Our task is to remain faithful until He does.

If you become discouraged with the direction of your day or your life, turn your thoughts and prayers to God. He is a God of possibility, not negativity. He will help you count your blessings instead of your hardships. And then, with a renewed spirit of optimism and hope, you can properly thank your Father in heaven for His blessings, for His love, and for His Son.

More Great Ideas About Disappointments

The enemy of our souls loves to taunt us with past failures, wrongs, disappointments, disasters, and calamities. And if we let him continue doing this, our life becomes a long and dark tunnel, with very little light at the end.

Charles Swindoll

The difference between winning and losing is how we choose to react to disappointment.

Barbara Johnson

The next time you're disappointed, don't panic and don't give up. Just be patient and let God remind you he's still in control.

Max Lucado

If your hopes are being disappointed just now, it means that they are being purified.

Oswald Chambers

Though our pain and our disappointment and the details of our suffering may differ, there is an abundance of God's grace and peace available to each of us.

Charles Swindoll

More from God's Word

I called to the Lord in my distress; I called to my God. From His temple He heard my voice.

2 Samuel 22:7 HCSB

But as for you, be strong; don't be discouraged, for your work has a reward.

2 Chronicles 15:7 HCSB

Consider it a great joy, my brothers, whenever you experience various trials, knowing that the testing of your faith produces endurance. But endurance must do its complete work, so that you may be mature and complete, lacking nothing.

James 1:2-4 HCSB

These things I have spoken to you, that in Me you may have peace. In the world you will have tribulation; but be of good cheer, I have overcome the world.

John 16:33 NKJV

For a righteous man may fall seven times and rise again.

Proverbs 24:16 NKJV

Now may the God of hope fill you with all joy and peace in believing, so that you may overflow with hope by the power of the Holy Spirit.

Romans 15:13 HCSB

Big Dreams

Are you willing to entertain the possibility that God has big plans in store for you? Hopefully so. Yet sometimes, especially if you've recently experienced a life-altering disappointment, you may find it difficult to envision a brighter future for yourself and your family. If so, it's time to reconsider your own capabilities . . . and God's.

Your Heavenly Father created you with unique gifts and untapped talents; your job is to tap them. When you do, you'll begin to feel an increasing sense of confidence in yourself and in your future.

It takes courage to dream big dreams. You will discover that courage when you do three things: accept the past, trust God to handle the future, and make the most of the time He has given you today.

Nothing is too difficult for God, and no dreams are too big for Him—not even yours. So start living—and dreaming—accordingly.

More Great Ideas About Dreams

Do we reach for nothing in life because our reaching opens us up to tragedy?

John Eldredge

You cannot out-dream God.

John Eldredge

To make your dream come true, you have to stay awake.

Dennis Swanberg

The future lies all before us. Shall it only be a slight advance upon what we usually do? Ought it not to be a bound, a leap forward to altitudes of endeavor and success undreamed of before?

Annie Armstrong

Sometimes our dreams were so big that it took two people to dream them.

Marie T. Freeman

More from God's Word

Where there is no vision, the people perish....

Proverbs 29:18 KJV

Be of good courage, and he shall strengthen your heart, all ye that hope in the LORD.

Psalm 31:24 KJV

Therefore, as we have opportunity, we must work for the good of all, especially for those who belong to the household of faith.

Galatians 6:10 HCSB

But as it is written: What no eye has seen and no ear has heard, and what has never come into a man's heart, is what God has prepared for those who love Him.

1 Corinthians 2:9 HCSB

Looking at them, Jesus said, "With men it is impossible, but not with God, because all things are possible with God."

Mark 10:27 HCSB

"Follow Me," Jesus told them, "and I will make you into fishers of men!" Immediately they left their nets and followed Him.

Mark 1:17-18 HCSB

Discipleship Now

When Jesus addressed His disciples, He warned that each one must "take up his cross and follow Me." The disciples must have known exactly what the Master meant. In Jesus' day, prisoners were forced to carry their own crosses to the location where they would be put to death. Thus, Christ's message was clear: in order to follow Him, Christ's disciples must deny themselves and, instead, trust Him completely. Nothing has changed since then.

If we are to be disciples of Christ, we must trust Him and place Him at the very center of our beings. Jesus never comes "next." He is always first. The paradox, of course, is that only by sacrificing ourselves to Him do we gain salvation for ourselves.

Do you seek to be a worthy disciple of Christ? Then pick up His cross today and every day that you live. When you do, He will bless you now and forever.

More Great Ideas About Discipleship

God is a place of safety you can run to, but it helps if you are running to Him on a daily basis so that you are in familiar territory.

Stormie Omartian

Our devotion to God is strengthened when we offer Him a fresh commitment each day.

Elizabeth George

You cannot cooperate with Jesus in becoming what He wants you to become and simultaneously be what the world desires to make you. If you would say, "Take the world but give me Jesus," then you must deny yourself and take up your cross. The simple truth is that your "self" must be put to death in order for you to get to the point where for you to live is Christ. What will it be? The world and you, or Jesus and you? You do have a choice to make.

Kay Arthur

When Jesus put the little child in the midst of His disciples, He did not tell the little child to become like His disciples; He told the disciples to become like the little child.

Ruth Bell Graham

More from God's Word

You did not choose Me, but I chose you. I appointed you that you should go out and produce fruit, and that your fruit should remain, so that whatever you ask the Father in My name, He will give you.

John 15:16 HCSB

But whoever keeps His word, truly in him the love of God is perfected. This is how we know we are in Him: the one who says he remains in Him should walk just as He walked.

1 John 2:5-6 HCSB

We encouraged, comforted, and implored each one of you to walk worthy of God, who calls you into His own kingdom and glory.

1 Thessalonians 2:12 HCSB

The one who loves his life will lose it, and the one who hates his life in this world will keep it for eternal life. If anyone serves Me, he must follow Me. Where I am, there My servant also will be. If anyone serves Me, the Father will honor him.

John 12:25-26 HCSB

When I was a child, I spoke as a child, I understood as a child, I thought as a child; but when I became a man, I put away childish things.

1 Corinthians 13:11 NKJV

Still Growing Up

The journey toward spiritual maturity lasts a lifetime. As Christians, we can and should continue to grow in the love and the knowledge of our Savior as long as we live. Norman Vincent Peale had the following advice for believers of all ages: "Ask the God who made you to keep remaking you." That advice, of course, is perfectly sound but often ignored.

When we cease to grow, either emotionally or spiritually, we do ourselves a profound disservice. But, if we study God's Word, if we obey His commandments, and if we live in the center of His will, we will not be "stagnant" believers; we will, instead, be growing Christians . . . and that's exactly what God intends for us to be.

Life is a series of choices and decisions. Each day, we make countless decisions that can bring us closer to God . . . or not. When we live according to the principles contained in God's Holy Word, we embark upon a journey of spiritual maturity that results in life abundant and life eternal.

More Great Ideas About Maturity

I've never met anyone who became instantly mature. It's a painstaking process that God takes us through, and it includes such things as waiting, failing, losing, and being misunderstood—each calling for extra doses of perseverance.

Charles Swindoll

Being a Christian means accepting the terms of creation, accepting God as our maker and redeemer, and growing day by day into an increasingly glorious creature in Christ, developing joy, experiencing love, maturing in peace.

Eugene Peterson

The disappointment has come, not because God desires to hurt you or make you miserable or to demoralize you, or ruin your life, or keep you from ever knowing happiness. He wants you to be perfect and complete in every aspect, lacking nothing. It's not the easy times that make you more like Jesus, but the hard times.

Kay Arthur

More from God's Word

Even a young man is known by his actions—by whether his behavior is pure and upright.

Proverbs 20:11 HCSB

So you may walk in the way of goodness, and keep to the paths of righteousness. For the upright will dwell in the land, and the blameless will remain in it.

Proverbs 2:20-21 NKJV

Now he who plants and he who waters are one, and each one will receive his own reward according to his own labor.

1 Corinthians 3:8 NKJV

You will show me the path of life; in Your presence is fullness of joy; at Your right hand are pleasures forevermore.

Psalm 16:11 NKJV

If you don't know what you're doing, pray to the Father. He loves to help. You'll get his help, and won't be condescended to when you ask for it. Ask boldly, believingly, without a second thought. People who "worry their prayers" are like wind-whipped waves. Don't think you're going to get anything from the Master that way, adrift at sea, keeping all your options open.

James 1:5-8 MSG

Rejoice always, pray without ceasing, in everything give thanks; for this is the will of God in Christ Jesus for you.

1 Thessalonians 5:16-18 NKJV

Be Thankful

For most of us, life is busy and complicated. We have countless responsibilities, some of which begin before sunrise and many of which end long after sunset. Amid the rush and crush of the daily grind, it is easy to lose sight of God and His blessings. But, when we forget to slow down and say "Thank You" to our Maker, we rob ourselves of His presence, His peace, and His joy.

Our task, as believing Christians, is to praise God many times each day. Then, with gratitude in our hearts, we can face our daily duties with the perspective and power that only He can provide.

More Great Ideas About Gratitude

Gratitude unlocks the fullness of life. It turns what we have into enough, and more. It turns denial into acceptance, chaos to order, confusion to clarity. It can turn a meal into a feast, a house into a home, a stranger into a friend. Gratitude makes sense of our past, brings peace for today, and creates a vision for tomorrow.

Melody Beattie

We become happy, spiritually prosperous people not because we receive what we want, but because we appreciate what we have.

Penelope Stokes

If you won't fill your heart with gratitude, the devil will fill it with something else.

Marie T. Freeman

It is only with gratitude that life becomes rich.

Dietrich Bonhoeffer

More from God's Word

Therefore as you have received Christ Jesus the Lord, walk in Him, rooted and built up in Him and established in the faith, just as you were taught, and overflowing with thankfulness.

Colossians 2:6-7 HCSB

Those who cling to worthless idols forsake faithful love, but as for me, I will sacrifice to You with a voice of thanksgiving. I will fulfill what I have vowed. Salvation is from the Lord!

Jonah 2:8-9 HCSB

Thanks be to God for His indescribable gift.

2 Corinthians 9:15 HCSB

And let the peace of the Messiah, to which you were also called in one body, control your hearts. Be thankful.

Colossians 3:15 HCSB

Give thanks to the Lord, for He is good; His faithful love endures forever.

Psalm 118:29 HCSB

So he who had received five talents came and brought five other talents, saying, "Lord, you delivered to me five talents; look, I have gained five more talents besides them." His lord said to him, "Well done, good and faithful servant; you were faithful over a few things, I will make you ruler over many things. Enter into the joy of your lord."

Matthew 25:20-21 NKJV

Using Your Talents

The old saying is both familiar and true: "What we are is God's gift to us; what we become is our gift to God." Each of us possesses special talents, gifted by God, that can be nurtured carefully or ignored totally. Our challenge, of course, is to use our abilities to the greatest extent possible and to use them in ways that honor our Savior.

Are you using your natural talents to make God's world a better place? If so, congratulations. But if you have gifts that you have not fully explored and developed, perhaps you need to have a chat with the One who gave you those gifts in the first place. Your talents are priceless treasures offered from your Heavenly Father. Use them. After all, an obvious way to say "thank you" to the Giver is to use the gifts He has given.

More Great Ideas About Talents

In the great orchestra we call life, you have an instrument and a song, and you owe it to God to play them both sublimely.

Max Lucado

You are the only person on earth who can use your ability.

Zig Ziglar

One thing taught large in the Holy Scriptures is that while God gives His gifts freely, He will require a strict accounting of them at the end of the road. Each man is personally responsible for his store, be it large or small, and will be required to explain his use of it before the judgment seat of Christ.

A. W. Tozer

The Lord is glad to open the gate to every knocking soul. It opens very freely; its hinges are not rusted, no bolts secure it. Have faith and enter at this moment through holy courage. If you knock with a heavy heart, you shall yet sing with joy of spirit. Never be discouraged!

C. H. Spurgeon

More from God's Word

Do not neglect the gift that is in you.

1 Timothy 4:14 HCSB

Each one has his own gift from God, one in this manner and another in that.

1 Corinthians 7:7 NKJV

I remind you to keep ablaze the gift of God that is in you.

2 Timothy 1:6 HCSB

Based on the gift they have received, everyone should use it to serve others, as good managers of the varied grace of God.

1 Peter 4:10 HCSB

According to the grace given to us, we have different gifts: If prophecy, use it according to the standard of faith; if service, in service; if teaching, in teaching; if exhorting, in exhortation; giving, with generosity; leading, with diligence; showing mercy, with cheerfulness.

Romans 12:6-8 HCSB

Immediately the father of the child cried out and said with tears, "Lord, I believe; help my unbelief!"

Mark 9:24 NKJV

Beyond the Doubts

E ven the most faithful Christians are overcome by occasional bouts of fear and doubt. You are no different. When you feel that your faith is being tested to its limits, seek the comfort and assurance of the One who sent His Son as a sacrifice for you.

Have you ever felt your faith in God slipping away? If so, you are not alone. Every life—including yours—is a series of successes and failures, celebrations and disappointments, joys and sorrows, hopes and doubts.

But even when you feel very distant from God, remember that God is never distant from you. When you sincerely seek His presence, He will touch your heart, calm your fears, and restore your soul.

More Great Ideas About Doubts

Doubting may temporarily disturb, but will not permanently destroy, your faith in Christ.

Charles Swindoll

A life lived in God is not lived on the plane of feelings, but of the will.

Elisabeth Elliot

Seldom do you enjoy the luxury of making decisions that are based on enough evidence to absolutely silence all skepticism.

Bill Hybels

Struggling with God over the issues of life doesn't show a lack of faith—that is faith.

Lee Strobel

Fear and doubt are conquered by a faith that rejoices. And faith can rejoice because the promises of God are as certain as God Himself.

Kay Arthur

More from God's Word

If you don't know what you're doing, pray to the Father. He loves to help. You'll get his help, and won't be condescended to when you ask for it. Ask boldly, believingly, without a second thought. People who "worry their prayers" are like wind-whipped waves. Don't think you're going to get anything from the Master that way, adrift at sea, keeping all your options open.

James 1:5-8 MSG

So He said, "Come." And when Peter had come down out of the boat, he walked on the water to go to Jesus. But when he saw that the wind was boisterous, he was afraid; and beginning to sink he cried out, saying, "Lord, save me!" And immediately Jesus stretched out His hand and caught him, and said to him, "O you of little faith, why did you doubt?" And when they got into the boat, the wind ceased.

Matthew 14:29-32 NKJV

Teach me, O Lord, the way of Your statutes, and I shall keep it to the end.

Psalm 119:33 NKJV

Don't abandon wisdom, and she will watch over you; love her, and she will guard you.

Proverbs 4:6 HCSB

Can you understand the secrets of God? His limits are higher than the heavens; you cannot reach them! They are deeper than the grave; you cannot understand them! His limits are longer than the earth and wider than the sea.

Job 11:7-9 NCV

He Reigns

God is sovereign. He reigns over the entire universe, and He reigns over your little corner of that universe. Your challenge is to recognize God's sovereignty, to live in accordance with His commandments, and to trust His promises. Sometimes, of course, these tasks are easier said than done.

Your Heavenly Father may not always reveal Himself as quickly (or as clearly) as you would like. But rest assured: God is in control, God is here, and God intends to use you in wonderful, unexpected ways. He desires to lead you along a path of His choosing. Your challenge is to watch, to listen, to learn . . . and to follow. Today.

More Great Ideas About
God's Sovereignty

As you place yourself under the sovereign lordship of Jesus Christ, each mistake or failure can lead you right back to the throne.

Barbara Johnson

Waiting is the hardest kind of work, but God knows best, and we may joyfully leave all in His hands.

Lottie Moon

He has the right to interrupt your life. He is Lord. When you accepted Him as Lord, you gave Him the right to help Himself to your life anytime He wants.

Henry Blackaby

Nothing happens by happenstance. I am not in the hands of fate, nor am I the victim of man's whims or the devil's ploys. There is One who sits above man, above Satan, and above all heavenly hosts as the ultimate authority of all the universe. That One is my God and my Father!

Kay Arthur

More from God's Word

For now we see indistinctly, as in a mirror, but then face to face. Now I know in part, but then I will know fully, as I am fully known.

1 Corinthians 13:12 HCSB

However, each one must live his life in the situation the Lord assigned when God called him.

1 Corinthians 7:17 HCSB

Notice the way God does things; then fall into line. Don't fight the ways of God.

Ecclesiastes 7:13 NLT

O Lord, you have examined my heart and know everything about me. You know when I sit down or stand up. You know my every thought when far away. You chart the path ahead of me and tell me where to stop and rest.

Psalm 139:1-3 NLT

Humble yourselves, therefore, under God's mighty hand, that he may lift you up in due time.

1 Peter 5:6 NIV

Let us lay aside every weight and the sin that so easily ensnares us, and run with endurance the race that lies before us, keeping our eyes on Jesus, the source and perfecter of our faith.

Hebrews 12:1-2 HCSB

Above the Daily Distractions

All of us must live through those days when the traffic jams, the computer crashes, and the dog makes a main course out of our homework. But, when we find ourselves distracted by the minor frustrations of life, we must catch ourselves, take a deep breath, and lift our thoughts upward.

Although we must sometimes struggle mightily to rise above the distractions of the everyday living, we need never struggle alone. God is here—eternal and faithful, with infinite patience and love—and, if we reach out to Him, He will restore our sense of perspective and give peace to our hearts.

Today, as an exercise in character-building, make this promise to yourself and keep it: promise to focus your thoughts on things that are really important, things like your faith, your family, your friends, and your future.

Don't allow the day's interruptions to derail your most important work. And don't allow other people (or, for that matter, the media) to decide what's important to you and your family.

Distractions are everywhere, but, thankfully, so is God . . . and that fact has everything to do with how you prioritize your day and your life.

Teach me, O Lord, the way
of Your statutes,
and I shall keep it to the end.

—

Psalm 119:33 NKJV

More Great Ideas About Distractions

Among the enemies to devotion, none is so harmful as distractions. Whatever excites the curiosity, scatters the thoughts, disquiets the heart, absorbs the interests, or shifts our life focus from the kingdom of God within us to the world around us—that is a distraction; and the world is full of them.

A. W. Tozer

Give me the person who says, "This one thing I do, and not these fifty things I dabble in."

D. L. Moody

The demand of every day kept me so busy that I subconsciously equated my busyness with commitment to Christ.

Vonette Bright

You can't get second things by putting them first; you can get second things only be putting first things first.

C. S. Lewis

We need to stop focusing on our lacks and stop giving out excuses and start looking at and listening to Jesus.

Anne Graham Lotz

Come to me, all you who are weary and burdened, and I will give you rest. Take my yoke upon you and learn from me, for I am gentle and humble in heart, and you will find rest for your souls. For my yoke is easy and my burden is light.

Matthew 11:28-30 NIV

Enough Rest?

Even the most inspired Christians can, from time to time, find themselves running on empty. The demands of daily life can drain us of our strength and rob us of the joy that is rightfully ours in Christ. When we find ourselves tired, discouraged, or worse, there is a source from which we can draw the power needed to recharge our spiritual batteries. That source is God.

God intends that His children lead joyous lives filled with abundance and peace. But sometimes, abundance and peace seem very far away. It is then that we must turn to God for renewal, and when we do, He will restore us.

God expects us to work hard, but He also intends for us to rest. When we fail to take the rest that we need, we do a disservice to ourselves, to our families, and others around us.

Is your spiritual battery running low? Is your energy on the wane? Are your emotions frayed? If so, it's time to turn your thoughts and your prayers to God. And when you're finished, it's time to rest.

Full of hope, you'll relax,
confident again; you'll look around,
sit back, and take it easy.

—

Job 11:18 MSG

More Great Ideas About Rest

Satan does some of his worst work on exhausted Christians when nerves are frayed and their minds are faint.

Vance Havner

Life is strenuous. See that your clock does not run down.

Mrs. Charles E. Cowman

Thou hast formed us for Thyself, and our hearts are restless till they find rest in Thee.

St. Augustine

Prescription for a happier and healthier life: resolve to slow down your pace; learn to say no gracefully; resist the temptation to chase after more pleasure, more hobbies, and more social entanglements.

James Dobson

Oh, the tranquil joy of that dear retreat, / Where the Savior bids thee rest, / With steadfast hope, and a trusting faith, / In His love secure and blest.

Fanny Crosby

Six days shall work be done, but the seventh day is a Sabbath of solemn rest, a holy convocation. You shall do no work on it; it is the Sabbath of the Lord in all your dwellings.

Leviticus 23:3 NKJV

Keeping the Sabbath

When God gave Moses the Ten Commandments, it became perfectly clear that our Heavenly Father intends for us to make the Sabbath a holy day, a day for worship, for contemplation, for fellowship, and for rest. Yet we live in a seven-day-a-week world, a world that all too often treats Sunday as a regular workday.

One way to strengthen your character is by giving God at least one day each week. If you carve out the time for a day of worship and praise, you'll be amazed at the impact it will have on the rest of your week. But if you fail to honor God's day, if you treat the Sabbath as a day to work or a day to party, you'll miss out on a harvest of blessings that is only available one day each week.

How does your family observe the Lord's day? When church is over, do you treat Sunday like any other day of the week? If so, it's time to think long and hard about your family's schedule and your family's priorities. And if you've been treating Sunday as just another day, it's time to break that habit. When Sunday rolls around, don't try to fill every spare moment. Take time to rest . . . Father's orders!

Worship the Lord with gladness.
Come before him, singing with joy.
Acknowledge that the Lord is God!
He made us, and we are his.
We are his people, the sheep
of his pasture.

—

Psalm 100:2-3 NLT

More Great Ideas About the Sabbath

Jesus taught us by example to get out of the rat race and recharge our batteries.

Barbara Johnson

Jesus gives us the ultimate rest, the confidence we need, to escape the frustration and chaos of the world around us.

Billy Graham

It is what Jesus is, not what we are, that gives rest to the soul. If we really want to overcome Satan and have peace with God, we must "fix our eyes on Jesus." Let his death, his suffering, his glories, and his intercession be fresh on your mind.

C. H. Spurgeon

One reason so much American Christianity is a mile wide and an inch deep is that Christians are simply tired. Sometimes you need to kick back and rest for Jesus' sake.

Dennis Swanberg

Come, come, come unto Me, / Weary and sore distressed; / Come, come, come unto Me, / Come unto Me and rest.

Fanny Crosby

Blessed are the poor in spirit, for theirs is the kingdom of heaven. Blessed are those who mourn, for they shall be comforted.

Matthew 5:3-4 NKJV

Sad Days

Some days are light and happy, and some days are not. When we face the inevitable dark days of life, we must choose how we will respond. Will we allow ourselves to sink even more deeply into our own sadness, or will we do the difficult work of pulling ourselves out? We bring light to the dark days of life by turning first to God, and then to trusted family members and friends. Then, we must go to work solving the problems that confront us. When we do, the clouds will eventually part, and the sun will shine once more upon our souls.

More Great Ideas About Sad Days

We are not called to be burden-bearers, but cross-bearers and light-bearers. We must cast our burdens on the Lord.

Corrie ten Boom

Feelings of uselessness and hopelessness are not from God, but from the evil one, the devil, who wants to discourage you and thwart your effectiveness for the Lord.

Bill Bright

What the devil loves is that vague cloud of unspecified guilt feeling or unspecified virtue by which he lures us into despair or presumption.

C. S. Lewis

There is no pit so deep that God's love is not deeper still.

Corrie ten Boom

In the soul-searching of our lives, we are to stay quiet so we can hear Him say all that He wants to say to us in our hearts.

Charles Swindoll

More from God's Word

Why are you cast down, O my soul? And why are you disquieted within me? Hope in God; for I shall yet praise Him, the help of my countenance and my God.

Psalm 42:11 NKJV

Then they cried out to the Lord in their trouble; He saved them from their distress.

Psalm 107:13 HCSB

I assure you: You will weep and wail, but the world will rejoice. You will become sorrowful, but your sorrow will turn to joy.

John 16:20 HCSB

May the God of hope fill you with all joy and peace as you trust in him, so that you may overflow with hope by the power of the Holy Spirit.

Romans 15:13 NIV

I have heard your prayer, I have seen your tears; surely I will heal you.

2 Kings 20:5 NKJV

Verse 89

The one who acquires good sense loves himself; one who safeguards understanding finds success.

Proverbs 19:8 HCSB

Perspective for Today

If a temporary loss of perspective has left you worried, exhausted, or both, it's time to readjust your thought patterns. Negative thoughts are habit-forming; thankfully, so are positive ones. With practice, you can form the habit of focusing on God's priorities and your own possibilities. When you do, you'll soon discover that you will spend less time fretting about your challenges and more time praising God for His gifts.

When you call upon the Lord and prayerfully seek His will, He will give you wisdom and perspective. When you make God's priorities your priorities, He will direct your steps and calm your fears. So today and every day hereafter, pray for a sense of balance and perspective. And remember: no problems are too big for God—and that includes yours.

More Great Ideas About Perspective

The proper perspective creates within us a spirit of reaching outside of ourselves with joy and enthusiasm.

Luci Swindoll

Like a shadow declining swiftly…away…like the dew of the morning gone with the heat of the day; like the wind in the treetops, like a wave of the sea, so are our lives on earth when seen in light of eternity.

Ruth Bell Graham

Earthly fears are no fears at all. Answer the big questions of eternity, and the little questions of life fall into perspective.

Max Lucado

Live near to God, and so all things will appear to you little in comparison with eternal realities.

Robert Murray McCheyne

Gratitude unlocks the fullness of life. It turns what we have into enough, and more. It turns denial into acceptance, chaos to order, confusion to clarity. It can turn a meal into a feast, a house into a home, a stranger into a friend. Gratitude makes sense of our past, brings peace for today, and creates a vision for tomorrow.

Melody Beattie

More from God's Word

Now if any of you lacks wisdom, he should ask God, who gives to all generously and without criticizing, and it will be given to him.

James 1:5 HCSB

For now we see in a mirror, dimly, but then face to face. Now I know in part, but then I shall know just as I also am known.

1 Corinthians 13:12 NKJV

Let no one deceive himself. If anyone among you seems to be wise in this age, let him become a fool that he may become wise. For the wisdom of this world is foolishness with God. For it is written, "He catches the wise in their own craftiness."

1 Corinthians 3:18-19 NKJV

Acquire wisdom—how much better it is than gold! And acquire understanding—it is preferable to silver.

Proverbs 16:16 HCSB

Don't abandon wisdom, and she will watch over you; love her, and she will guard you.

Proverbs 4:6 HCSB

For am I now trying to win the favor of people, or God? Or am I striving to please people? If I were still trying to please people, I would not be a slave of Christ.

Galatians 1:10 HCSB

Choosing to Please God

Whom will you try to please today: God or man? Your primary obligation is not to please imperfect men and women. Your obligation is to strive diligently to meet the expectations of an all-knowing and perfect God.

Sometimes, because you're an imperfect human being, you may become so wrapped up in meeting society's expectations that you fail to focus on God's expectations. To do so is a mistake of major proportions—don't make it. Instead, seek God's guidance as you focus your energies on becoming the best "you" that you can possibly be. And, when it comes to matters of conscience, seek approval not from your peers, but from your Creator.

More Great Ideas About Pleasing God

A heart out of tune, out of sync with God's heart, will produce a life of spiritual barrenness and missed opportunities.

Jim Cymbala

Make God's will the focus of your life day by day. If you seek to please Him and Him alone, you'll find yourself satisfied with life.

Kay Arthur

You must never sacrifice your relationship with God for the sake of a relationship with another person.

Charles Stanley

All our offerings, whether music or martyrdom, are like the intrinsically worthless present of a child, which a father values indeed, but values only for the intention.

C. S. Lewis

It is impossible to please God doing things motivated by and produced by the flesh.

Bill Bright

More from God's Word

Therefore, whether we are at home or away, we make it our aim to be pleasing to Him.

2 Corinthians 5:9 HCSB

For you were once darkness, but now you are light in the Lord. Walk as children of light—for the fruit of the light results in all goodness, righteousness, and truth—discerning what is pleasing to the Lord.

Ephesians 5:8-10 HCSB

But I will hope continually and will praise You more and more.

Psalm 71:14 HCSB

So you may walk in the way of goodness, and keep to the paths of righteousness. For the upright will dwell in the land, and the blameless will remain in it.

Proverbs 2:20-21 NKJV

The one who pursues righteousness and faithful love will find life, righteousness, and honor.

Proverbs 21:21 HCSB

Praise the Lord! Oh, give thanks to the Lord, for He is good!
For His mercy endures forever.

Psalm 106:1 NKJV

Praise Him

Because we have been saved by God's only Son, we must never lose hope in the priceless gifts of eternal love and eternal life. And, because we are so richly blessed, we must approach our Heavenly Father with reverence and thanksgiving.

Sometimes, in our rush "to get things done," we simply don't stop long enough to pause and thank our Creator for the countless blessings He has bestowed upon us. But when we slow down and express our gratitude to the One who made us, we enrich our own lives and the lives of those around us.

Thanksgiving should become a habit, a regular part of our daily routines. God has blessed us beyond measure, and we owe Him everything, including our eternal praise. Let us praise Him today, tomorrow, and throughout eternity.

More Great Ideas About Praise

Nothing we do is more powerful or more life-changing than praising God.

Stormie Omartian

What happens when we praise the Father? We reestablish the proper chain of command.

Max Lucado

Two wings are necessary to lift our souls toward God: prayer and praise. Prayer asks. Praise accepts the answer.

Mrs. Charles E. Cowman

Most of the verses written about praise in God's Word were voiced by people faced with crushing heartaches, injustice, treachery, slander, and scores of other difficult situations.

Joni Eareckson Tada

Be not afraid of saying too much in the praises of God; all the danger is of saying too little.

Matthew Henry

More from God's Word

From the rising of the sun to its going down the Lord's name is to be praised.

Psalm 113:3 NKJV

Enter into His gates with thanksgiving, and into His courts with praise. Be thankful to Him, and bless His name. For the Lord is good; His mercy is everlasting, and His truth endures to all generations.

Psalm 100:4-5 NKJV

So that at the name of Jesus every knee should bow—of those who are in heaven and on earth and under the earth—and every tongue should confess that Jesus Christ is Lord, to the glory of God the Father.

Philippians 2:10-11 HCSB

But I will hope continually, and will praise You yet more and more.

Psalm 71:14 NKJV

In everything give thanks; for this is the will of God in Christ Jesus for you.

2 Thessalonians 5:18 NKJV

Blessed is the man who walks not in the counsel of the ungodly, nor stands in the path of sinners, nor sits in the seat of the scornful; but his delight is in the law of the Lord, and in His law he meditates day and night.

Psalm 1:1-2 NKJV

Walking with the Righteous

Peer pressure can be a good thing or a bad thing, depending upon your peers. If your peers encourage you to make integrity a habit—and if they encourage you to follow God's will and to obey His commandments—then you'll experience positive peer pressure, and that's good. But, if you are involved with people who encourage you to do foolish things, you're facing a wrong kind of peer pressure . . . beware. When you feel pressured to do things, or to say things, that lead you away from God, you're aiming straight for trouble.

Are you satisfied to follow that crowd? If so, you may pay a heavy price unless you've picked the right crowd. And while you're deciding whom to follow, be sure you're determined to follow the One from Galilee, too. Jesus will guide your steps and bless your undertakings if you let Him. Your challenge, of course, is to let Him.

To sum it up, here's your choice: you can choose to please God first (and by doing so, strengthen your character), or you can fall prey to peer pressure. The choice is yours—and so are the consequences.

He who walks with wise men will be wise, but the companion of fools will be destroyed.

—

Proverbs 13:20 NKJV

More Great Ideas About Peer Pressure

For better or worse, you will eventually become more and more like the people you associate with. So why not associate with people who make you better, not worse?

Marie T. Freeman

You must never sacrifice your relationship with God for the sake of a relationship with another person.

Charles Stanley

It is impossible to please God doing things motivated by and produced by the flesh.

Bill Bright

You should forget about trying to be popular with everybody and start trying to be popular with God Almighty.

Sam Jones

Do you want to be wise? Choose wise friends.

Charles Swindoll

Thanks be to God for His indescribable gift.

2 Corinthians 9:15 HCSB

A Thankful Heart

Sometimes, life here on earth can be complicated, demanding, and frustrating. When the demands of life leave us rushing from place to place with scarcely a moment to spare, we may fail to pause and thank our Creator for the countless blessings He bestows upon us. But, whenever we neglect to give proper thanks to the Giver of all things good, we suffer because of our misplaced priorities.

As believers who have been saved by a risen Christ, we are blessed beyond human comprehension. We who have been given so much should make thanksgiving a habit, a regular part of our daily routines. Of course, God's gifts are too numerous to count, but we should attempt to count them nonetheless. We owe our Heavenly Father everything, including our eternal praise . . . starting right now.

More Great Ideas About Thanksgiving

God has promised that if we harvest well with the tools of thanksgiving, there will be seeds for planting in the spring.

Gloria Gaither

It is always possible to be thankful for what is given rather than to complain about what is not given. One or the other becomes a habit of life.

Elisabeth Elliot

The joy of the Holy Spirit is experienced by giving thanks in all situations.

Bill Bright

The words "thank" and "think" come from the same root word. If we would think more, we would thank more.

Warren Wiersbe

God often keeps us on the path by guiding us through the counsel of friends and trusted spiritual advisors.

Bill Hybels

More from God's Word

And let the peace of the Messiah, to which you were also called in one body, control your hearts. Be thankful.

Colossians 3:15 HCSB

Therefore as you have received Christ Jesus the Lord, walk in Him, rooted and built up in Him and established in the faith, just as you were taught, and overflowing with thankfulness.

Colossians 2:6-7 HCSB

It is good to give thanks to the Lord, and to sing praises to Your name, O Most High.

Psalm 92:1 NKJV

Enter into His gates with thanksgiving, and into His courts with praise. Be thankful to Him, and bless His name. For the Lord is good; His mercy is everlasting, and His truth endures to all generations.

Psalm 100:4-5 NKJV

And whatever you do, in word or in deed, do everything in the name of the Lord Jesus, giving thanks to God the Father through Him.

Colossians 3:17 HCSB

Then the One seated on the throne said, "Look! I am making everything new."

Revelation 21:5 HCSB

New Beginnings

I f we sincerely want to change ourselves for the better, we must start on the inside and work our way out from there. Lasting change doesn't occur "out there"; it occurs "in here." It occurs, not in the shifting sands of our own particular circumstances, but in the quiet depths of our own hearts.

Life is constantly changing. Our circumstances change; our opportunities change; our responsibilities change; and our relationships change. When we reach the inevitable crossroads of life, we may feel the need to jumpstart our lives . . . or the need to start over from scratch.

Are you in search of a new beginning or, for that matter, a new you? If so, don't expect changing circumstances to miraculously transform you into the person you want to become. Transformation starts with God, and it starts in the silent center of a humble human heart—like yours.

More Great Ideas About
New Beginnings

God is not running an antique shop! He is making all things new!

Vance Havner

The amazing thing about Jesus is that He doesn't just patch up our lives, He gives us a brand new sheet, a clean slate to start over, all new.

Gloria Gaither

Like a spring of pure water, God's peace in our hearts brings cleansing and refreshment to our minds and bodies.

Billy Graham

Whoever you are, whatever your condition or circumstance, whatever your past or problem, Jesus can restore you to wholeness.

Anne Graham Lotz

Walking with God leads to receiving his intimate counsel, and counseling leads to deep restoration.

John Eldredge

More from God's Word

But those who wait on the Lord shall renew their strength; they shall mount up with wings like eagles, they shall run and not be weary, they shall walk and not faint.

Isaiah 40:31 NKJV

Therefore if anyone is in Christ, he is a new creature; the old things passed away; behold, new things have come.

2 Corinthians 5:17 HCSB

You are being renewed in the spirit of your minds; you put on the new man, the one created according to God's likeness in righteousness and purity of the truth.

Ephesians 4:23-24 HCSB

I will give you a new heart and put a new spirit within you.

Ezekiel 36:26 HCSB

Therefore, this is what the Lord says: If you return, I will restore you; you will stand in My presence.

Jeremiah 15:19 HCSB

Teach me, O Lord, the way of Your statutes, and I shall keep it to the end.

Psalm 119:33 NKJV

Still Learning

Whether you're twenty-two or a hundred and two, you've still got lots to learn. Even if you're a very wise person, God isn't finished with you yet. Why? Because lifetime learning is part of God's plan—and He certainly hasn't finished teaching you some very important lessons.

Do you seek to live a life of righteousness and wisdom? If so, you must continue to study the ultimate source of wisdom: the Word of God. You must associate, day in and day out, with godly men and women. And, you must act in accordance with your beliefs. When you study God's Word and live according to His commandments, you will become wise . . . and you will be a blessing to your friends, to your family, and to the world.

More Great Ideas About Wisdom

God's plan for our guidance is for us to grow gradually in wisdom before we get to the crossroads.

Bill Hybels

If you lack knowledge, go to school. If you lack wisdom, get on your knees.

Vance Havner

Wisdom takes us beyond the realm of mere right and wrong. Wisdom takes into account our personalities, our strengths, our weaknesses, and even our present state of mind.

Charles Stanley

All the knowledge you want is comprised in one book, the Bible.

John Wesley

A big difference exists between a head full of knowledge and the words of God literally abiding in us.

Beth Moore

More from God's Word

The fear of the Lord is the beginning of wisdom; a good understanding have all those who do His commandments. His praise endures forever.

Psalm 111:10 NKJV

Therefore, everyone who hears these words of Mine and acts on them will be like a sensible man who built his house on the rock. The rain fell, the rivers rose, and the winds blew and pounded that house. Yet it didn't collapse, because its foundation was on the rock.

Matthew 7:24–25 HCSB

A wise man will hear and increase learning, and a man of understanding will attain wise counsel.

Proverbs 1:5 NKJV

So teach us to number our days, that we may gain a heart of wisdom.

Psalm 90:12 NKJV

Acquire wisdom—how much better it is than gold! And acquire understanding—it is preferable to silver.

Proverbs 16:16 HCSB

And you shall know the truth, and the truth shall make you free.

John 8:32 NKJV

Truth with a Capital T

God is vitally concerned with truth. His Word teaches the truth; His Spirit reveals the truth; His Son leads us to the truth. When we open our hearts to God, and when we allow His Son to rule over our thoughts and our lives, God reveals Himself, and we come to understand the truth about ourselves and the Truth (with a capital T) about God's gift of grace.

The familiar words of John 8:32 remind us that when we come to know God's Truth, we are liberated. Have you been liberated by that Truth? And are you living in accordance with the eternal truths that you find in God's Holy Word? Hopefully so.

Today, as you fulfill the responsibilities that God has placed before you, ask yourself this question: "Do my thoughts and actions bear witness to the ultimate Truth that God has placed in my heart, or am I allowing the pressures of everyday life to overwhelm me?" It's a profound question that deserves an answer . . . now.

More Great Ideas About Truth

For Christians, God himself is the only absolute; truth and ethics are rooted in his character.

Charles Colson

Truth will triumph. The Father of truth will win, and the followers of truth will be saved.

Max Lucado

Having a doctrine pass before the mind is not what the Bible means by knowing the truth. It's only when it reaches down deep into the heart that the truth begins to set us free, just as a key must penetrate a lock to turn it, or as rainfall must saturate the earth down to the roots in order for your garden to grow.

John Eldredge

If the price of which you shall have a true experience is that of sorrow, buy the truth at that price.

C. H. Spurgeon

Only Jesus Christ is the truth for everyone who has ever been born into the human race, regardless of culture, age, nationality, generation, heritage, gender, color, or language.

Anne Graham Lotz

Do not love the world or the things in the world. If anyone loves the world, the love of the Father is not in him.

1 John 2:15 NKJV

The World's Treasures or God's Treasures?

All of mankind is engaged in a colossal, world-wide treasure hunt. Some folks seek treasure from earthly sources, treasures such as material wealth or public acclaim; others seek God's treasures by making Him the cornerstone of their lives.

What kind of treasure hunter are you? Are you so caught up in the demands of popular society that you sometimes allow the search for worldly treasures to become your primary focus? If so, it's time to reorganize your daily to-do list by placing God in His rightful place: first place.

If you sincerely seek to strengthen your character, you'll focus more intently on God's treasures and less intently on the world's treasures. Don't allow anyone or anything to separate you from your Heavenly Father and His only begotten Son.

Society's priorities are transitory; God's priorities are permanent. The world's treasures are difficult to find and difficult to keep; God's treasures are ever-present and ev-erlasting. Which treasures and whose priorities will you claim as your own? The answer should be obvious.

More Great Ideas About Worldliness

Every day, I find countless opportunities to decide whether I will obey God and demonstrate my love for Him or try to please myself or the world system. God is waiting for my choices.

Bill Bright

Too many Christians have geared their program to please, to entertain, and to gain favor from this world. We are concerned with how much, instead of how little, like this age we can become.

Billy Graham

Tell me that you love the world, and I will tell you that love of the world is enmity to God.

C. H. Spurgeon

Aim at heaven and you will get earth thrown in; aim at earth and you will get neither.

C. S. Lewis

For I am the Lord, I do not change.

Malachi 3:6 NKJV

He Does Not Change

O ur world is in a state of constant change. God is not. At times, the world seems to be trembling beneath our feet. But we can be comforted in the knowledge that our Heavenly Father is the rock that cannot be shaken. His Word promises, "I am the Lord, I do not change."

Every day that we live, we mortals encounter a multitude of changes—some good, some not so good. And on occasion, all of us must endure life-changing personal losses that leave us heartbroken. When we do, our Heavenly Father stands ready to comfort us, to guide us, and—in time—to heal us.

Is the world spinning a little too fast for your liking? Are you facing difficult circumstances or unwelcome changes? If so, please remember that God is far bigger than any problem you may face. So, instead of worrying about life's inevitable challenges, put your faith in the Father and His only begotten Son. After all, "Jesus Christ is the same yesterday, today, and forever" (Hebrews 13:8 NKJV). And it is precisely because your

Savior does not change that you can face your challenges with courage for today and hope for tomorrow.

Are you anxious about situations that you cannot control? Take your anxieties to God. Are you troubled? Take your troubles to Him. Does your little corner of the universe seem to be trembling beneath your feet? Seek protection from the One who cannot be moved. The same God who created the universe will protect you if you ask Him . . . so ask Him . . . and then serve Him with willing hands and a trusting heart.

*Love the Lord your God with
all your heart, with all your soul,
and with all your strength.*

—

Deuteronomy 6:5 HCSB

More Great Ideas About God

God is bigger than we can figure.

Criswell Freeman

God does not tell us what He is going to do; He reveals to us who He is.

Oswald Chambers

God's actual divine essence and his will are absolutely beyond all human thought, human understanding or wisdom; in short, they are and ever will be incomprehensible, inscrutable, and altogether hidden to human reason.

Martin Luther

The God who dwells in heaven is willing to dwell also in the heart of the humble believer.

Warren Wiersbe

God can see clearly no matter how dark or foggy the night is. Trust His Word to guide you safely home.

Lisa Whelchel

You are the light of the world. A city that is set on a hill cannot be hidden. Nor do they light a lamp and put it under a basket, but on a lampstand, and it gives light to all who are in the house. Let your light so shine before men, that they may see your good works and glorify your Father in heaven.

Matthew 5:14-16 NKJV

You Are the Light

Matthew 5:14-16 makes it clear: Because you are a Christian, you are indeed "the light of the world." The Bible also says that you should live in a way that lets other people understand what it means to be a follower of Jesus.

Your personal testimony is profoundly important, but perhaps because of shyness (or because of the fear of being rebuffed), you've been hesitant to share your experiences. If so, you should start paying less attention to your own insecurities and more attention to the message that God wants you to share with the world.

Corrie ten Boom observed, "There is nothing anybody else can do that can stop God from using us. We can turn everything into a testimony." Her words remind us that when we speak up for God, our actions may speak even more loudly than our words.

When we let other people know the details of our faith, we assume an important responsibility: the responsibility of making certain that our words are reinforced by our actions. When we share our testimonies, we must also be willing to serve as shining examples of righteousness—undeniable examples of the changes that Jesus makes in the lives of those who accept Him as their Savior.

Are you willing to follow in the footsteps of Jesus? If so, you must also be willing to talk about Him. And make no mistake—the time to express your belief in Him is now. You know how He has touched your own heart; help Him do the same for others.

Proclaim the message; persist in it whether convenient or not; rebuke, correct, and encourage with great patience and teaching.

2 Timothy 4:2 HCSB

More Great Ideas About Witnessing

Stay on the issue of Christ when witnessing, not the church, or denominations, or religion, or theological differences, or doctrinal questions. Speak precisely of Jesus, the Savior.

Charles Swindoll

Every tiny bit of my life that has value I owe to the redemption of Jesus Christ. Am I doing anything to enable Him to bring His redemption into evident reality in the lives of others?

Oswald Chambers

Jesus' images portray the Kingdom as a kind of secret force. Sheep among wolves, treasure hidden in a field, the tiniest seed in a garden, wheat growing among weeds, a pinch of yeast worked into bread dough; all these hint at a movement that works within society, changing it from inside out.

Philip Yancey

There is no thrill quite as wonderful as seeing someone else come to trust Christ because I have been faithful in sharing the story of my own faith.

Vonette Bright

Whoever serves me must follow me. Then my servant will be with me everywhere I am. My Father will honor anyone who serves me.

John 12:26 NCV

Following His Footsteps

Each day, we make countless decisions that can bring us closer to God...or not. When we live according to God's commandments, we reap bountiful rewards: abundance, hope, and peace, for starters. But, when we turn our backs upon God by disobeying Him, we bring needless suffering upon ourselves and our families.

Do you seek to walk in the footsteps of the One from Galilee, or will you choose another path? If you sincerely seek God's peace and His blessings, then you must strive to imitate God's Son.

Thomas Brooks spoke for believers of every generation when he observed, "Christ is the sun, and all the watches of our lives should be set by the dial of his motion." Christ, indeed, is the ultimate Savior of mankind and the personal Savior of those who believe in Him. As His servants, we should walk in His footsteps as we share His love and His message with a world that needs both.

More Great Ideas About Imitating Christ

Every Christian is to become a little Christ. The whole purpose of becoming a Christian is simply nothing else.

C. S. Lewis

Prayer makes a godly man and puts within him "the mind of Christ," the mind of humility, of self-surrender, of service, and of piety. If we really pray, we will become more like God, or else we will quit praying.

E. M. Bounds

The steady discipline of intimate friendship with Jesus results in men becoming like Him.

Harry Emerson Fosdick

You cannot cooperate with Jesus in becoming what He wants you to become and simultaneously be what the world desires to make you. If you would say, "Take the world but give me Jesus," then you must deny yourself and take up your cross. The simple truth is that your "self" must be put to death in order for you to get to the point where for you to live is Christ. What will it be? The world and you, or Jesus and you? You do have a choice to make.

Kay Arthur

More from God's Word

Therefore, be imitators of God, as dearly loved children.

Ephesians 5:1 HCSB

But whoever keeps His word, truly the love of God is perfected in him. By this we know that we are in Him. He who says he abides in Him ought himself also to walk just as He walked.

1 John 2:5-6 NKJV

Then Jesus spoke to them again: "I am the light of the world. Anyone who follows Me will never walk in the darkness, but will have the light of life."

John 8:12 HCSB

Christ's life showed me how, and enabled me to do it. I identified myself completely with him. Indeed, I have been crucified with Christ. My ego is no longer central. It is no longer important that I appear righteous before you or have your good opinion, and I am no longer driven to impress God. Christ lives in me. The life you see me living is not "mine," but it is lived by faith in the Son of God, who loved me and gave himself for me.

Galatians 2:20 MSG